Yahweh's Spacecraft

BY

GARY WENDELL STANFIELD SR.

©2025 Gary Wendell Stanfield Sr. All rights reserved.

No part of this publication may be reproduced, distributed, or transmitted in any form or by any means, including photocopying, recording, or other electronic or mechanical methods, without the prior written permission of the publisher, Parker Publishers, except in the case of brief quotations embodied in critical reviews and certain other non-commercial uses permitted by copyright law.

For permission requests, write to the author, addressed to:

Gary Wendell Stanfield Sr.

DEDICATION

I dedicate this book to Uptight (Michael Aultman), a person that I met years ago on Christian Chat and the name he went by. We hit it off from the beginning. We are still friends today. I remember a time when he started talking about spacecraft, and he wondered about the thoughts I had about them. I remember telling him that I know the scriptures speak about spacecraft but that I had never done a study on them. He told me to study them, and I did. I made two or three different studies about them, so I have combined them for this book and even authored a poem about 'Yahweh's Spacecraft from the information given and found in the scriptures. I know he was a firm believer in their existence. Then, it made me think about why I never did a study on them. After all, my studies are all about finding the truth to the lies and cover-ups of Christianity. Now that I know why I never did, it was because of a group called ""Heaven's Gate"," a new religious cult movement at that time that had committed mass suicides in 1997 and was started in 1974 by a Marshall Applewhite that was still fresh in my mind. I figured people would think that I belonged to that group, and in reality, a few did after I had done my first study. Then it hit me that would make people not believe the truth about spacecraft and write anyone off who even mentioned them. After all, they are taught White horses are going to ride through space, and they also believe reindeer fly. That made me even more focused on studying them the best I could with the proof from the scriptures. Then in the last couple weeks in November of 2024, I figured I would go ahead and produce a book on them from what the scriptures really teach and all the verses that I had compiled on them. I give all the Credit for the making of this book to Uptight; Christians cannot comprehend spacecraft, though those who are really searching for truth have accepted it once they see the compiled truth. I even had a few Christians apologize to me for how they had treated me, coming against that teaching, yet when they searched it out, they could see it was true. This world needs a wake-up call! Too many are comfortable with believing that they are going to heaven, and that is also a Christian lie, as are so many other subjects that they teach as truth. So Uptight it was you that planted that seed in my mind that has produced this book and why this Dedication is to you only.

PREFACE

This book is based on the verses that prove spacecraft, making it the main topic of this book to bring spacecraft to the forefront, even though there are other studies added within this book to further educate people about the truth. You do not hear any teaching about them within Christianity outside of the Christian Church teachings. Those who do speak on spacecraft only mention them from the book of Ezekiel and nowhere else where they are spoken of and used in scripture. They are spoken about all through the scriptures, and they are used by Yahweh Messiah, and they really do exist. It is what is written within the content of the pages to teach and educate to make a learning experience for those who take the time to read and study it. Books like this one are used for education on this subject matter to make people more knowledgeable in their learning process of studying to receive from what is on the pages and used to bring the study of spacecraft to make people become more aware of their existence, Just because Christianity as a whole will not teach about them if they did it would end the coming back on a white horse teaching. Just another hidden truth of scriptures in Christianity and why it is taught that Jesus Christ, an Anti- Messiah name, is coming back riding a White Horse, but Yahweh Messiah is coming in spacecraft. What they want you to believe these are extraterrestrial Aliens. Never believe that lie. **I'M SURE MORE VERSES PERTAINING TO SPACECRAFT CAN BE FOUND. I 'DON'T HAVE THEM ALL.**

Psalm 68:17

17. The Chariots of Yahweh are twenty thousand, even thousands of Messengers: Yahweh is among them, as in Sinai, in the righteous place.

Studies done by Gary Wendell Stanfield Sr.

All poems written by Gary W. Stanfield Sr.

Table of Contents

CHAPTER 1 'YAHWEH'S SPACECRAFT 2
CHAPTER 2 SATAN KICKED OUT OF HEAVEN IN SPACECRAFT. 6
CHAPTER 3 PROOF OF 'YAHWEH'S HEAVEN, 'MAN'S EARTH 14
CHAPTER 4 TOWER OF BABEL – YAHWEH CAME DOWN 16
CHAPTER 5 PROOF YAHWEH USES SPACECRAFT 18
CHAPTER 6 THE CHERUB/CHERUBIM 21
CHAPTER 7 THE STAR 26
CHAPTER 8 MESSENGERS ARE MEN IN HUMAN FORM 29
CHAPTER 9 TRANSFIGURATION 32
CHAPTER 10 THOSE THAT WERE AND WILL BE TAKEN UP 37
CHAPTER 11 WHAT HAPPENS DURING THE ARMAGEDDON WAR WITH SPACECRAFT 40
CHAPTER 12 HIS THRONE 42
CHAPTER 13 PHILLIP TRANSPORTED 47
CHAPTER 14 PAUL ON THE ROAD TO DAMASCUS 48
CHAPTER 15 JOHN OF REVELATION WAS TAKEN UP INTO A SPACECRAFT 51
CHAPTER 16 SECOND GOG AND MAGOG WAR: 52
CHAPTER 17 INTO THE CATCHING-UP SPACECRAFT 56
CHAPTER 18 PART 1 NEW ZION 64
CHAPTER 19 ELIJAH – ELISHA 68
CHAPTER 20 JUDAEA FLEEING EGYPT 70
CHAPTER 21 ELISHA AND THE CHARIOTS OF FIRE 82
CHAPTER 22 ELIJAH TAKEN UP IN A CHARIOT OF FIRE 84
CHAPTER 23 RONALD REAGAN AND ALIENS SPEECH 87
CHAPTER 24 ARMAGEDDON WAR – YAHWEH USES SPACECRAFT 91
CHAPTER 25 THEY HAVE BEEN HID FROM THE NEWER GENERATIONS: 94
CHAPTER 26 VERSES OF DECEIT: 96

CHAPTER 27 THE KINGDOM OF YAHWEH 98
CHAPTER 28 ZION IS THE HARLOT: 101
CHAPTER 29 VERSES WITH JUDAEA AND OTHER WORDS CORRECTED: SO, COMPARE 121
CHAPTER 30 #2 NEW ZION 126
CHAPTER 31 HEALINGS ARE COMING 129
CHAPTER 32 MARIAM'S LINEAGE: 131
CHAPTER 33 TIMELINE OF IMMANUEL 134
CHAPTER 34 SION MEANS THE SUN; ZION IS THE CITY 138
CHAPTER 35 THE NEW HEAVEN AND EARTH 143
CHAPTER 36 SATAN REPLACED WITH DEVIL, DEVILS; DEMON, DEMONS; UNCLEAN SPIRITS, EVIL SPIRITS 146
CHAPTER 37 THE END TIME - TIMELINE: 155
CHAPTER 38 HOMOSEXUALITY: 161
CHAPTER 39 GREED 173
CHAPTER 40 JOSEPH AND MARIAM TOOK A BOAT TO EGYPT 178
CHAPTER 41 THE OLIVET DISCOURSE ON BOTH TRIBULATION PERIODS 183
CHAPTER 42 HOW THE MESSIAH FULFILLED THE SPRING FEAST 186
CHAPTER 43 WHERE MAN ORIGINATED AT 195
CHAPTER 44 ALL ABOUT FATHER 204

Brainwashed

"When your mind has been programmed to believe certain things, your mind is also programmed to reject anything that teaches against them.

By Gary W. Stanfield

CHAPTER 1

'YAHWEH'S SPACECRAFT

""THE MESSIAH 'YOU'RE EXPECTING WILL NEVER COME"."

Revelation 19:11

"And I saw heaven opened and behold a white horse [spacecraft]; and he that sat on/WITHIN it *was* called Faithful and True, and in righteousness he doth judge and make war"." Horses cannot ride through space and why humans and even monkeys must have space suits to go into space. To fit another Christian lie.

Humans or anything that breaths ascend higher into the atmosphere, air density declines, which results in death from lack of oxygen the higher into the atmosphere a person or anything that draws breath will eventually die the higher they go, just like a horse would, and why there are such things as spacecraft. Christianity teaches that Christians will be raptured straight to heaven, meeting their Jesus in the sky and going to heaven with him. The truth is that 'Yahweh's Elect will be ""caught up"" in his spacecraft by his Messengers, which then will take the people to the mothership where they praise Yahweh Messiah in his throne room. The Mothership will be humongous.

Yahweh's Spacecraft

Yahweh returns in spacecraft, and all the wheat will be caught up into them,

The ones that are saved from Yahweh's wrath, those who had served Him.
Then Yahweh and His Messengers like birds flying, burns up all the chaff.
People never dreamed that all this will be done with Yahweh's spacecraft.

After this a great voice of many people in heaven and praising Yahweh,
For avenging the blood of His Elect, while the smoke ascended their way.
They are in spacecraft in heaven above the Earth, when this praise is done.
Then the Elect come right back to this Earth with Yahweh Messiah, the Son.

During His Kingdom, Yahweh teaches all those who never heard His Word,
Between Constantine's time and the 7-year Peace Plan with minds blurred.
That died in Satan's world, infested with our forefather's pagan lies,
Those who did not believe and turned the truth of Yahweh under a guise.

The whole truth will be taught during the 7-Year Peace Plan, be ready for it.
The miracles and healings once again, just like in the Acts so don't quit.
Want a spaceship ride, then Yahweh is the Messiah for those who survive?
From that day forward, you will never have to die, forever and eternally alive!

THE MESSIAH, 'THAT'S COMING YOU NEVER EXPECTED:

'Yahweh's Spacecraft

What they are calling 'UFOs are spacecraft and are of Yahweh and of Satan. Satan was kicked out of heaven to this Earth in them and not allowed to go back when Yahweh Messiah went back to heaven in a spacecraft.

Spacecraft in scriptures are spoken of as the Star, a cloud or clouds, chariots, chariots of fire, white horse, horses, Cherub, and Cherubin.

What I want to do is prove by the scriptures that spacecraft are real. Yahweh Messiah is returning in a spacecraft and not riding on a White Horse as Christianity teaches. I will show the scenarios with spacecraft involved within the scriptures.

Used with permission by J. Francis.

I met Mr. Francis on Christian Chat, and I was talking to him about 'Yahweh's spacecraft. During our conversation, he showed me this cartoon that he had made. I said something like you may have made it a cartoon, but if you only knew how true it is. Then I asked him if I could use it with my spacecraft study and he told me yes that I could and why I have chosen it to use on this book cover too. I hope someday he sees it since I forget where he was from. Many thanks go to him for the usage of it.

CHAPTER 2

SATAN KICKED OUT OF HEAVEN IN SPACECRAFT.

Revelation. 12:7-9

7. And there was war in heaven: Michael and his Messengers fought against the dragon; and the dragon fought and his messengers,

8. And prevailed not; neither was their place found any more in heaven.

9. And the great dragon was cast out, that old serpent, called SATAN which deceiveth the whole world: he was cast out into the Earth, and his messengers were cast out with him.

This war happened when Yahweh Messiah went back to heaven after telling his disciples that Satan was coming and he had nothing in him. This was a spacecraft war in the heavens. When Yahweh returns to wipe out the armies that came against Zion, Satan and his Messengers will be there to help them fight Yahweh at his coming, and this is when Yahweh will kill Satan and his messengers; Satan is in the grave during the Millennial Kingdom of Yahweh at its end is when Satan is raised up to deceive the world one last time, those people that had died after Constantine killed off the last of Yahweh 'Messiah's Elect and all the way up to the coming 7-Year 'Papacy's Peace Plan that will end WW3 that never heard the whole truth will be taught during the Millennium by Yahweh himself.

Mark 13:25-27

25 And the stars of heaven shall fall, and the powers that are in heaven shall be shaken.

26 And then shall they see the Son of man coming in the clouds with great power and righteousness.

""The stars of heaven shall fall"" – I believe these are 'Satan's spacecraft destroyed at 'Yahweh's coming. Satan will fight Yahweh at his coming. The U.S. now has a space force, so humanity may have a part in the fight in heaven at his return; the armies on Earth will fight him at his return to this Earth.

Revelation 20:1-3.7-9

1 And I saw a Messenger come down from heaven, (in a spacecraft) having the key of the bottomless pit and a great chain in his hand.

2 And he laid hold on the dragon, that old serpent, which is Satan, and bound him a thousand years,

3 And cast him into the bottomless pit, and shut him up, and set a seal upon him, that he should deceive the nations no more, till the thousand years should be fulfilled: and after that he must be loosed a little season.

7 And when the thousand years are expired, Satan shall be loosed out of his prison,

8 And shall go out to deceive the nations which are in the four quarters of the Earth, Gog and Magog,(there are 2 Gog Magog wars) to gather them together to battle: the number of whom *is* as the sand of the sea.

9 And they went up on the breadth of the Earth, and compassed the camp of the Elect about, and the beloved city: and fire came down from Yahweh out of heaven and devoured them.

10 And SATAN that deceived them was cast into the lake of fire and brimstone, where the beast and the false prophet *are*.

And shall be tormented – EVEN SATAN WILL BURN UP, NOT EVEN SATAN BURNS FOREVER AND EVER.

""and shall be tormented day and night forever and ever"." THIS LAST PART WAS ADDED; NO ONE BURNS FOREVER AND EVER NOT EVEN SATAN, ANOTHER CHRISTIAN LIE.

Malachi 4:1

For, behold, the day cometh, that shall burn as an oven; and all the proud, yea, and all that do wickedly, shall be stubble: and the day that cometh shall burn them up, saith Yahweh of hosts, that it shall leave them neither root nor branch.

The 3 heavens:

(1) Our Immediate Atmosphere,

(2) Outer Space (The Sun, Moon, And Stars)

(3) The highest Heaven, The Home of Yahweh; 'YAHWEH'S DOMAIN. POSITIVELY SATAN IS NOT ALLOWED.

Ephesians 4:10

He that descended is the same also that ascended far above all heavens, that he might fill all things.)

Isaiah 14:14

I will ascend above the heights of the clouds; I will be like the most High.

Revelation 12:9

""And the great dragon was cast out, that old serpent, called Satan, which deceiveth the whole world: he was cast out into the earth, and his messengers were cast out with him"."

Luke 10:18

""I beheld Satan as lightning fall from heaven"." Revelation 12:12 Therefore rejoice, ye heavens, and ye that dwell in them. Woe to the inhabiters of the Earth and of the sea! for Satan has come down unto you, having great wrath, because he knoweth that he hath but a short time.

1 Peter 5:8 - Be sober, be vigilant; because your adversary Satan, as a roaring lion, walketh about, seeking whom he may devour:

1 John 3:8 He that committeth transgression is of Satan; for Satan transgresses from the beginning. For this purpose, the Son of Yahweh was manifested, that he might destroy the works of Satan.

2 Corinthians 11:14 And no marvel; for Satan himself is transformed into a messenger of light.

John 8:44 Ye are of your father Satan, and the lusts of your father ye will do. He was a murderer from the beginning, and abode not in the truth, because there is no truth in him. When he speaketh a lie, he speaketh of his own: for he is a liar, and the father of it.

You can see why Christianity is of Satan speaking his lies.

James 4:7 Submit yourselves therefore to Yahweh. Resist Satan, and he will flee from you.

John 10:10 The thief cometh not, but for to steal, and to kill, and to destroy: I have come that they might have life, and that they might have it more abundantly.

2 Corinthians 11:3 But I fear, lest by any means, as the serpent beguiled Eve through his subtilty, so your minds should be corrupted from the simplicity that is in Yahweh.

Romans 16:20 And Yahweh of peace shall bruise Satan under his feet shortly. The Spirit of our Master Yahweh Messiah be with you.

YAHWEH DID NOT COME TO BRING PEACE TO THIS WORLD, ONLY TO THOSE THAT SERVED HIM AND WERE FILLED WITH HIS SPIRIT, HIS ELECT. PEACE FOR THIS EARTH WILL BE DURING THE MILLENNIAL KINGDOM WHEN YAHWEH RULES.

Revelation 12:9 - And the great dragon was cast out, that old serpent, called Satan, which deceiveth the whole world: he was cast out into the Earth, and his messengers were cast out with him.

TOWER OF BABEL – Yahweh came down in a spacecraft

GENESIS 11: 5-7

⁵ And Yahweh came down to see the city and the tower, which the children of men built.

⁶ And Yahweh said, Behold, the people is one, and they have all one language; and this they begin to do: and now nothing will be restrained from them, which they have imagined doing.

⁷ Go to, let us go down, and there confound their language, that they may not understand one another's speech.

He came down in a spacecraft.

JOB 1:6-7

6 Now there was a day when the sons of Yahweh came to present themselves before Yahweh, and Satan came also among them.

7 And Yahweh said unto Satan, Whence comest thou? Then Satan answered Yahweh, and said, From going to and fro in the Earth, and from walking up and down in it.

SATAN USED SPACECRAFT TO GO BACK AND FORTH.

Matthew 4:8

Again, Satan taketh him up into an exceeding high mountain, and sheweth him all the kingdoms of the world, and the esteem of them;

The above verse happened before Satan was kicked out of heaven to this Earth and not allowed to ever return. Not only that, but there is no mountain high enough that they could have gone up on to see all the kingdoms of the world, even those back then. This is just a thought on how it was done, 'Satan's spacecraft TOOK THEM UP ABOVE THE EARTH TO SEE ALL THE KINGDOMS or on some type of monitor on a spacecraft.

2 Corinthians 4:4 –

In whom the mighty one of this world hath blinded the minds of them which believe not, lest the light of the righteous Word of Yahweh, who is the image of Yahweh, should shine unto them.

John 1:1-2

1 In the beginning was the Word, and the Word was with Yahweh, and the Word was Yahweh.

2 The same was in the beginning with Yahweh.

With the above two verses, anyone can answer the question in Proverbs 30:4: Who hath ascended up into heaven, or descended? Who hath gathered the wind in his fists? Who hath bound the waters in a garment? Who hath established all the ends of the Earth? What is his name, and what is his son's name, if thou canst tell?

For those who can't, the answer is ""Yahweh"".

Luke 10:18 - And he said unto them, I beheld Satan as lightning fall from heaven. He fell in a spacecraft to this Earth, most likely running from 'Yahweh's armies, then not allowed back in heaven.

SATAN WAS CONFINED TO THIS EARTH IN THE OLD COVENANT BUT STILL ALLOWED TO GO BACK AND FORTH ACCUSING PEOPLE. HE WAS KICKED OUT PERMANENTLY WHEN THE MESSIAH WENT BACK. YAHWEH WILL KILL HIM DURING THE ARMAGEDDON WAR, WHERE HE WILL BE DEAD FOR 1000 YEARS. YAHWEH WILL RAISE HIM AT THE END OF THOSE THOUSAND YEARS SO SATAN CAN DECEIVE THOSE THAT WERE TAUGHT BY YAHWEH DURING THE MILLENIAL KINGDOM. SATAN THEN FIGHTS YAHWEH WITH ALL THE WICKED DURING THE 2ND GOG AND MAGOG WAR, AND THAT IS THE JUDGEMENT WAR.

WHERE SATAN AND HIS FOLLOWERS ARE BURNED UP WITH THIS EARTH, AND NONE OF THEM WILL EVER EXIST AGAIN, THIS IS THE *WHITE* THRONE JUDGEMENT AFTER THE MILLENNIAL KINGDOM. THEN YAHWEH CREATES A NEW HEAVEN AND A NEW EARTH, WHERE HE WILL LIVE WITH HIS ELECT. AS YOU CAN SEE, SATAN HAS ALWAYS BEEN A LOSER, AND HE NEVER LEARNED THAT FACT.

THE FOLLOWING VERSES ARE NOW, WE ARE LIVING IN 'SATAN'S WORLD.

1 John 5:19 - And we know that we are of Yahweh, and the whole world lieth in wickedness.

Ephesians 6:12 - ""For we wrestle not against flesh and blood, but against principalities, against powers, against the rulers of the darkness of this world, against spiritual wickedness in high *places*"."

John 10:10 - The thief cometh not, but for to steal, and to kill, and to destroy: I am come that they might have life, and that they might have it more abundantly.

SOUNDS JUST LIKE THIS EARTH TODAY!

CHAPTER 3

PROOF OF 'YAHWEH'S HEAVEN, 'MAN'S EARTH

The 3 heavens:

(1) Our Immediate Atmosphere,

(2) Outer Space (The Sun, Moon, And Stars)

(3) The Home Of Yahweh; 'YAHWEH'S DOMAIN. SATAN IS NOT ALLOWED.

WHY PEOPLE GOING TO HEAVEN IS A CHRISTIAN LIE.

Isaiah 45:18

18 For thus saith Yahweh that created the heavens; <u>Yahweh himself that formed the Earth and made it</u>; he hath established it, he created it not in vain, <u>he formed it to be inhabited</u>: I am Yahweh; and there is none else.

Isaiah 45:12

12 **<u>I have made the Earth, and created man upon it</u>: I, even my hands, have stretched out the heavens,** and all their host have I commanded.

Revelation 21

21 And <u>I saw a new heaven and a new earth</u>: for the first heaven and the first Earth were passed away; and there was no more sea.

THE NEW EARTH IS WHERE HE WILL LIVE WITH HIS ELECT, NOT IN HEAVEN.

Psalms 24:1 <u>The Earth is Yahweh's, and the fulness thereof; the world, and they that dwell therein.</u>

This is speaking of his Millennial Kingdom or the New Earth

CHAPTER 4
TOWER OF BABEL – YAHWEH CAME DOWN

We know now that the Earth was made for man and the heavens were made for Yahweh, and he used spacecraft to go back and forth from the 3rd heaven to Earth and vice versa.

THE STORY ABOUT THE BUILDING OF THE TOWER OF BABEL:

Genesis 11: 1-9

1 And the whole Earth was of one language, and of one speech.

2 And it came to pass, as they journeyed from the East, that they found a plain in the land of Shinar; and they dwelt there.

3 And they said one to another, **3 Go to, let us make brick, and burn them throughly. And they had brick for stone, and slime had they for morter.**

4 And they said, Go to, let us build us a city and a tower, whose top may reach unto heaven; and let us make us a name, lest we be scattered abroad upon the face of the whole Earth.

5 And **Yahweh came down to see the city and the tower, which the children of men built.**

6 And <u>Yahweh said, Behold, the people *is* one, and they have all one language; and this they begin to do: and now nothing will be restrained from them, which they have imagined to do.</u>

7 Go to, **let us go down, and there confound their language, that they may not understand one another's speech.**

Yahweh came down in a spacecraft.

8 So Yahweh scattered them abroad from thence upon the face of all the Earth: and they left off to build the city.

Yahweh did not destroy the tower but changed their language, they quit building the tower.

9 Therefore is the name of it called Babel; because Yahweh did there confound the language of all the Earth: and from thence did Yahweh scatter them abroad upon the face of all the Earth.

CHAPTER 5

PROOF YAHWEH USES SPACECRAFT

Isaiah 68:4

4. <u>Sing unto Yahweh, sing praises to His name:</u> **extol him that rideth upon the heavens by his name Yahweh,** and rejoice before him.

Psalms 68: 4-5,7- 8 – Yahweh in a spacecraft.

⁴ Sing unto Yahweh, sing praises to his name: **extol him that rideth upon the heavens by his name Yahweh, and rejoice before him.**

⁵ A father of the fatherless, and a judge of the widows, **is Yahweh in his righteous habitation.**

⁷ **O Yahweh, when thou wentest forth before thy people, when thou didst march through the wilderness;** Selah:

⁸ The Earth shook, the heavens also dropped at the presence of Yahweh: even Sinai itself was moved at the presence of Yahweh, the Mighty One of Judah of Judaea.

Daniel 7:13 I saw in the night visions, and, **behold, one like the Son of man came with the clouds of heaven, and came to the Ancient of days,** and they brought him near before him.

2 Samuel 22:10-12

10. He bowed the heavens also and came down; and darkness was under his feet.

11. **And he rode upon a cherub, and did fly: and he was seen upon the wings of the wind.**

12. And **he made darkness pavilions round about him, dark waters, and thick clouds of the skies.**

Psalm 68:17

17. **The Chariots of Yahweh are twenty thousand, even thousands of Messengers: Yahweh is among them, as in Sinai**, in the righteous place.

Mark 13:24-27

24 But in those days, **after that tribulation**, the sun shall be darkened, and the moon shall not give her light.

25 And **the stars of heaven shall fall, and the powers that are in heaven shall be shaken.**

""the stars of heaven shall fall"" - Another way you could say that is, ""the space-craft of heaven coming down"".""

26 And **then shall they see the Son of man coming in the clouds/spacecraft with great power and righteousness.**

27 And **then shall he send his Messengers, and shall gather his Elect from the four winds, from the uttermost part of the Earth to the uttermost part of heaven.**

Psalms 18:9-11

9. **He bowed the heavens also and came down: and darkness was under his feet.**

10. **And He rode upon a cherub, and did fly: yea, He did fly upon the wings of the wind.**

11. He made darkness his secret place; his pavilion round about him were dark waters and thick clouds of the skies.

John 8:23 <u>I am not of this world</u>.

Psalms 104:3 <u>Who layeth the beams of his chambers in the waters: who maketh the clouds his chariot: who walketh upon the wings of the wind.</u>

Spacecraft have been seen going in and out of large bodies of water.

Revelation 1:7 Behold**, he cometh with clouds; and every eye shall see him, and they also which pierced him: and all kindreds of the Earth shall wail because of him.**

Matthew 16:27 For **the Son of man shall come in the righteousness of his Father with his Messengers;** and then he shall reward every man according to his works.

Coming in spacecraft

Deuteronomy 33:26

26 There is none like unto Yahweh of Jeshurun/Judaea, <u>who rideth upon the heaven in thy help, and in his excellency on the sky</u>

Psalms 18:9 **He bowed the heavens also, and came down: and darkness was under his feet.**

Zechariah 1:16 <u>Therefor thus saith Yahweh; I am returned to Zion with mercies: my House shall be built in it, saith Yahweh of hosts,</u> <u>and a line shall be stretched forth upon Zion.</u>

<u>Not only does this prove that Yahweh is returning in spacecraft but also that the ""House of Yahweh"" is rebuilt after his return.</u>

CHAPTER 6

THE CHERUB/CHERUBIM

Cherub is singular for whatever these things are, which seem to be a special type of spacecraft; cherubin is plural when speaking of more than one of them. Messengers are in human form that operate these things. Right now, there seems to be a lot of lack of knowledge about them.

Psalm 80:11

11 Give ear, O Shepherd of Judaea, thou that leadest Joseph like a flock; thou that dwellest between the cherubims, shine forth.

2 Chronicles 3:11

11 And the wings of the cherubim's were twenty cubits long: one wing of the one cherub was five cubits, reaching to the wall of the House: and the other wing was likewise five cubits, reaching to the wing of the other cherub.

11. And he rode upon a cherub, and did fly: and he was seen upon the wings of the wind.

Ezekiel 10:3-10

3 Now **the cherubim stood on the right side of the House of Yahweh, when the man went in; and the cloud filled the inner court.**

4 Then **the righteousness of Yahweh went up from the cherub and *stood* over the threshold of the House; and the House was filled with the cloud, and the court was full of the brightness of Yahweh's righteousness.**

5 And **the sound of the cherubim' wings was heard** even **to the outer court, as the voice of the Almighty Yahweh when he speaketh.**

6 And it came to pass, *that* when he had commanded the man clothed with linen, saying, **take fire from between the wheels, from between the cherubim; then he went in, and stood beside the wheels.**

7 And **one cherub stretched forth his hand from between the cherubim unto the fire that** *was* **between the cherubim, and took** *thereof,* **and put** *it* **into the hands of** *him that was* **clothed with linen: who took** *it and* **went out.**

8 And **there appeared in the cherubim the form of a man's hand under their wings.**

9 And **when I looked, behold the four wheels by the cherubim, one wheel by one cherub, and another wheel by another cherub: and the appearance of the wheels** *was* **as the color of a beryl stone.**

10 And *as for* their appearances, they four had one likeness, as if a wheel had been in the midst of a wheel.

Genesis 3:24 - THIS VERSE SPEAKS OF CHERABIM (PLURAL) IT HAS TO BE SPACECRAFT OF SOME KIND.

²⁴ **After he drove the man out, he placed on the east side of the Garden of Eden cherubim and a flaming sword flashing back and forth to guard the way to the tree of life.**

There was posted more than one Cherub to keep them out of the garden.

Isaiah 66:15 For, behold, **Yahweh will come with fire, and with his chariots like a whirlwind, to render his anger with fury, and his rebuke with flames of fire.**

Psalm 104:3 and **lays the beams of his upper chambers on their waters**.

He makes the clouds his chariot and rides on the wings of the wind.

Ezekiel 1:28

As the appearance of the bow that is in the cloud in the day of rain, so was the appearance of the brightness round about. This was the appearance of the likeness of the righteousness of Yahweh. **And when I saw it, I fell upon my face, and I heard a voice of one that spake.**

Ezekiel Chapter 10 describes spacecraft also, the "cherubim" are the smaller ones which are called horses too.

1 Then I looked, and behold, **in the firmament that was above the head of the cherubim there appeared over them as it were a sapphire stone, as the appearance of the likeness of a throne.**

2 And he spake unto the man clothed with linen, and said, **go in between the wheels, *even* under the cherub, and fill thine hand with coals of fire from between the cherubim,** and scatter *them* over the city. And he went in in my sight.

Ezekiel 10:11-22

11 When they went, they went upon their four sides; they turned not as they went, but to the place whither the head looked they followed it; they turned not as they went.

12 And their whole body, and their backs, and their hands, and their wings, and the wheels, *were* full of eyes round about, *even* the wheels that they four had.

13 **As for the wheels, it was cried unto them in my hearing, O wheel.**

14 **And everyone had four faces: the first face *was* the face of a cherub, and the second face *was* the face of a man, and the third the face of a lion, and the fourth the face of an eagle.**

15 And **the cherubim were lifted up. This** *is* **the living creature that I saw by the river of Chebar.**

16 And **when the cherubim went, the wheels went by them: and when the cherubim lifted up their wings to mount up from the Earth, the same wheels also turned not from beside them.**

17 **When they stood,** *these* **stood; and when they were lifted up,** *these* **lifted up themselves** *also*: **for the Spirit of the living creature** *was* **in them.**

18 Then **the righteousness of Yahweh departed from off the threshold of the House and stood over the cherubim.**

19 And **the cherubim lifted up their wings and mounted up from the Earth in my sight: when they went out, the wheels also** *were* **beside them, and** *everyone* **stood at the door of the east gate of Yahweh's House; and the righteousness of Yahweh of Judaea** *was* **over them above.**

20 This *is* **the living creature that I saw under Yahweh of Judaea by the river of Chebar; and I knew that they** *were* **the cherubim.**

21 **Everyone had four faces apiece, and everyone four wings; and the likeness of the hands of a man** *was* **under their wings.**

22 And **the likeness of their faces** *was* **the same faces which I saw by the river of Chebar, their appearances and themselves: they went everyone straight forward.**

To me the above verses is describing some type of spacecraft with Messengers inside which are in human form.

Psalm 80:1 Give ear, O Shepherd of Judaea, thou that leadest Joseph like a flock; thou that dwellest between the cherubims, shine forth.

CLOUDS, CHARIOTS, HORSES, WHIRLWIND, and SERAPHIMS are other representations of spacecraft. HORSES are the smaller ones that come out of a bigger CHARIOT or Mother Ship.

Job 38:1 Then **Yahweh answered Job out of the whirlwind**, and said,

CHAPTER 7

THE STAR

'Let's start when the wise men came to Zion first. Now, when they saw the Star, they were taken to Zion, not Bethlehem, where Immanuel was born. This was done so Herod would fulfill the prophecy of killing all the male children 2 years and younger. The wise men left Zion and went to Bethlehem of Galilee to find Immanuel living in a house, not a manger, and he was 2 years old, a toddler, not a baby. They showed up 2 years after 'Immanuel's birth. They were not at the manger scene like Christianity teaches.

Matthew 2:16-18

16. Then **Herod, when he saw that he was mocked of the wise men, was exceeding wroth, and sent forth, and slew all the children that were in Bethlehem, and in all the coasts thereof, from two years old and under, according to the time which he had diligently inquired of the wise men.**

17. **Then was fulfilled that which was spoken by Jeremiah the prophet, saying,**

18. **In Rama was there a voice heard, lamentation, and weeping, and great mourning, Rachel weeping for her children, and would not be comforted, because they are not.**

Now, to prove what the Star was:

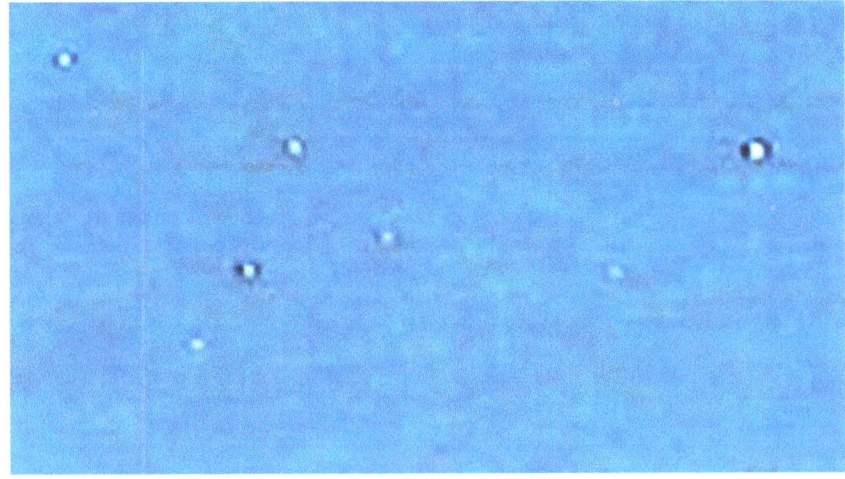

These are spacecraft, not stars; when they are high in the sky, they look like stars, and the lower they go, you can see what they are.

Matthew 2:1

1. Now when **Immanuel was born in Bethlehem of Galilee in the days of Herod the king, behold, there came wise men from the East to Zion,**

2. Saying, where is he that is born King of the Jews: for **we have seen his Star in the East and come to worship him**.

Notice here, they've seen the Star; the Star did not lead them to Bethlehem, where Immanuel was born, but to Zion first, then to Bethlehem of Galilee.

7. Then**erdz**

Notice the Star did not exist until it appeared.

9. When they had heard the king, they departed; and, **lo, the Star**, which they saw in the East, **WENT BEFORE THEM. Till IT CAME and STOOD OVER where the young child was.**

Notice here that the Star, when they departed appeared to them again and went before them and took them to the very House Immanuel was living in.

10. **When they saw the Star, they rejoiced with exceeding great joy.**

Why were they exceedingly joyous when they saw the Star and saw what it really was.

A star can lead you in a direction. It cannot move, so you can follow it. It cannot take you to a specific location. It wasn't until they came to the House and saw what they thought looked like a star was a spacecraft and why they were joyous when they saw it.

Messengers came down in a spacecraft and went back to heaven again in it.

Luke 2:8-10

8 And there were in the same country shepherds abiding in the field, keeping watch over their flock by night.

9 And, lo, **the Messenger of Yahweh came upon them, and the righteousness of Yahweh shone round about them:** and they were sore afraid.

10 And **the Messenger said unto them, Fear not: for, behold, I bring you good tidings of great joy, which shall be to all people.**

Luke 2:15 And it came to pass, as the Messengers were gone away from them into heaven, the shepherds said one to another, let us now go even unto Bethlehem, and see this thing, which has come to pass, which Yahweh hath made known unto us.

The Messengers went to heaven in a spacecraft.

CHAPTER 8

MESSENGERS ARE MEN IN HUMAN FORM

Daniel 9:21

Yea, whiles I *was* speaking in prayer, even **the man Gabriel,** whom I had seen in the vision at the beginning, **being caused to fly swiftly, touched me** about the time of the evening oblation.

18 Now as **he was speaking with me,** I was in a deep sleep on my face toward the ground: but and set me **he touched me and set me upright.**

Hebrews 13:2

2 **Be not forgetful to entertain strangers: for thereby some have entertained Messengers unawares.**

PROVES THAT THEY LOOK LIKE US WITHOUT WINGS.

Daniel 10:5-6

5 **Then I lifted mine eyes, and looked, and behold a certain man** clothed in linen, whose loins *were* girded with fine gold of Uphaz:

18 Then there came again and touched me **one like the appearance of a man**, and he strengthened me,

Hebrews 2:9

But we see **Immanuel, who was made a little lower than the Messengers for the suffering of death,** crowned with righteousness and honour; that he by the Spirit of Yahweh should taste death for every man.

Judges 6:21-22

21 **Then the Messenger of Yahweh put forth the end of the staff that *was* in his hand,** and touched the flesh and the unleavened cakes; and there rose up fire out of the rock, and consumed the flesh and the unleavened cakes. Then **the Messenger of Yahweh** departed out of his sight.

22 And when **Gideon perceived that he *was* an Messenger of Yahweh,** Gideon said, Alas, O Yahweh! for because **I have seen a Messenger of Yahweh face to face.**

Genesis 19:3-4,10,12,16

3 And he pressed upon them greatly; and they turned in unto him, and entered into his House; and he made them a feast, and did bake unleavened bread, and **they did eat.**

4 But **before they lay down**, the men of the city, *even* the men of Sodom, compassed the house round, both old and young, all the people from every quarter:

10 **But the men put forth their hand, and pulled Lot into the House to them, and shut to the door.**

12 And **the men said** unto Lot, Hast thou here any besides? son in law, and thy sons, and thy daughters, and whatsoever thou hast in the city, bring *them* out of this place:

16 And while he lingered, **the men laid hold upon his hand, and upon the hand of his wife, and upon the hand of his two daughters;** Yahweh being merciful unto him: and **they brought him forth,** and set him without the city.

Joshua 5:13-15

¹³ And it came to pass, **when Joshua was by Jericho, that he lifted up his eyes and looked, and, behold, there stood a man over against him with his sword drawn in his hand: and Joshua went unto him, and said unto him, Art thou for us, or for our adversaries?**

¹⁴ And **he said, Nay; but as captain of the host of Yahweh am I now come. And Joshua fell on his face to the Earth, and did worship, and said unto him, What saith my Master unto his servant?**

¹⁵ And **the captain of Yahweh's host said unto Joshua, Loose thy shoe from off thy foot; for the place whereon thou standest is righteous. And Joshua did so.**

This Messenger is the Captain of 'Yahweh's Messenger Army.

Joshua 6:1-2,27 **1 Now Jericho was straitly shut up because of the children of Judaea: none went out, and none came in.**

2 And **Yahweh said unto Joshua, See, I have given into thine hand Jericho, and the king thereof, and the mighty men of valour.**

27 So **Yahweh WAS WITH JOSHUA; AND HIS FAME WAS NOISED THROUGHOUT ALL THE COUNTRY.**

The verses above show Yahweh spoke to Joshua, so he was there too.

MESSENGERS CANNOT DIE, WHERE IMMANUEL DID DIE. THEY DO NOT HAVE WINGS.

Hebrews 13:2 ² **Be not forgetful to entertain strangers: for thereby some have entertained Messengers unawares.**

CHAPTER 9
TRANSFIGURATION

Matthew 6:28

Verily I say unto you, **there be some standing here, which shall not taste of death, till they see the Son of man coming in his kingdom.**

Mark 9:1

And he said unto them, Verily I say unto you, **that there be some of them that stand here, which shall not taste of death, till they have seen the kingdom of Yahweh come with power.**

Mark 9:2

After six days **Immanuel took Peter, James and John with him and led them up a high mountain, where they were all alone. There he was transfigured before them.**

It was Peter, James, and John of whom he was speaking about who would not see death till they see him coming in his kingdom.

Luke 9:28-36 tells the same story as Matthew and Mark.

In Luke 9:34 it brings out something that Matthew and Mark do not say.

34. While he thus spake, **THERE CAME A CLOUD, and OVERSHADOWED THEM: and THEY FEARED as THEY ENTERED INTO THE CLOUD.**

Mothership hiding in the clouds

A spacecraft can completely engulf itself in a cloud. They can make their own clouds to hide in.

NOTICE: **It shows that THEY ENTERED THIS CLOUD, they entered the spacecraft, CAUGHT UP IN THE CLOUDS. INSIDE SPACECRAFT.**

Matthew 17:1-3, 5, **Matthew 17:1-9 tells the whole story.**

1. And after six days **Immanuel taketh Peter, James and John his brother, and bringeth them into a high mountain apart,**

2. And <u>**was transfigured before them**</u>: and <u>**his face did shine as the sun, and his raiment was white as the light.**</u>

6 days later after Immanuel said that some standing there would not see death until they have seen the Kingdom of Yahweh. Immanuel was transfigured and his face shined as the sun and his raiment was as white as the light. This is his righteousness being revealed. His righteousness gives the light to New Zion. THEY SEEN HIM TRANSFORM FROM A CELESTIAL TO A TERRESTRIAL BODY AND SEEN MOSES AND ELIJAH IN A RESURRECTED STATE, THEY BOTH HAD DIED, CONTRARY TO CHRISTIAN TEACHING, THE KINGDOM OF YAHWEH IS SPIRITUAL.

TO PROVE THIS:

LUKE 2:9 And, lo, the Messenger of Yahweh came upon them, and the righteousness of Yahweh shone round about them: and they were sore afraid.

MESSENGERS ARE SPIRIT FILLED ALSO, WITH RIGHTEOUSNESS.

Revelation 21: 23-24

23 And the city had no need of the sun, neither of the moon, to shine in it: for the righteousness of Yahweh did lighten it, and the Lamb is the light thereof.

24 And the nations of them which are saved shall walk in the light of it: and the kings of the earth do bring their righteousness and honor into it.

ISAIAH 26:2 Open ye the gates, that the righteous nation which keepeth the truth may enter in.

The true Messiah did not have long hair; the halo comes from pagan sun worship.

Mark 9:1-8 tells the same story as Matthew and Luke do.

3. And, behold, there appeared unto them Moses and Elijah talking with him.

5. While he yet spake, behold, **A BRIGHT CLOUD OVERSHADOWED THEM: and behold A VOICE OUT OF THE CLOUD, which said, This is my beloved Son, in whom I am well pleased, hear ye him.**

The cloud is a spacecraft.

Acts 1:9-11

9. And when he had spoken these things, while they beheld, **HE WAS TAKEN UP**; and **a CLOUD RECEIVED HIM** out of their sight. **He returned to heaven.**

1 Timothy 3:16 KJV states: "And without controversy great is the mystery of righteousness: Yahweh was manifest in the flesh, justified in the Spirit, seen of Messengers, taught unto the Gentiles, believed on in the world, **received up into heaven.**"

A cloud received him, a spacecraft that took him to heaven.

LUKE 24:51

""And it came to pass, while he blessed them, **he was parted from them and carried up into heaven**"."

10. And while **they looked steadfastly toward heaven as he went up**, behold, **two men stood by them in white apparel**;

11. Which also said, Ye men of Galilee, **why stand ye gazing up into heaven? This same Yahweh, which is taken up from you into heaven, shall so come in like manner as ye have seen him go into heaven.**

A spacecraft took him up, and he will return in a spacecraft.

Mark 14:62

And Immanuel said, I am and ye shall see the Son of man sitting on the right hand of power and **COMING IN THE CLOUDS OF HEAVEN.**

Daniel 7:13 I saw in the night visions, and behold, **one like the Son of man came with the clouds of heaven,** and came to the Ancient of days, and they brought him near before him.

Notice it says: **Coming in the clouds, not coming on the clouds? They are SPACECRAFT!**

Let's compare when the Messiah was taken up in a cloud (singular) in Acts 1:9 and 1 Thessalonians 4:17 when the Elect are received up into CLOUDS (plural), and the two witnesses taken up in a CLOUD (singular).

CHAPTER 10

THOSE THAT WERE AND WILL BE TAKEN UP

A.) THE MESSIAH IS TAKEN UP IN A CLOUD/ A SPACECRAFT.

Acts 1:9-11

9. And when he had spoken these things, while they beheld, **he was taken up; and a CLOUD RECEIVED HIM out of their sight.**

B.) A POST-TRIBULATION ""CATCHING UP"" TAKEN UP INTO SPACECRAFT:

C.) THE TWO WITNESSES ARE TAKEN UP IN A CLOUD.

Revelations 11:12

12. And **they heard a great voice from heaven saying unto them, come up hither,** and **they ASCENDED UP TO HEAVEN IN A CLOUD**; and their enemies beheld them.

Yes, the cloud and clouds are the spacecraft of Yahweh. As you can see, the Messiah, two witnesses, and the true believers are taken up INTO A CLOUD AND CLOUDS.

Isaiah 66:15

15. For, behold, **Yahweh will come with fire, and with his chariots like a whirlwind, to render his anger with fury, and his rebuke with flames of fire.**

CHAPTER 11
WHAT HAPPENS DURING THE ARMAGEDDON WAR WITH SPACECRAFT

Mark 13:26-27

26. And **then shall they see the Son of man coming IN (not on) the clouds** with great power and esteem.

27. And **then shall he send his Messengers and shall gather together his Elect from the four winds, from the uttermost part of the Earth to the uttermost part of heaven.**

This is my favorite picture showing a mothership and the Messenger crafts leaving it or returning. THE CHARIOT AND ITS HORSES SPOKEN OF IN SCRIPTURES.

The Messengers will collect the Elect in their crafts and take them to the mothership where Yahweh's throne is and where the Elect are worshipping Yahweh above the Earth in the mothership throne room.

Daniel 9:9 I beheld till the thrones were cast down, and the Ancient of days did sit, whose garment was white as snow, and the hair of his head like the pure wool: **his throne was like the fiery flame, and his wheels as burning fire.**

A Spacecraft Mothership

CHAPTER 12

HIS THRONE

Matthew 5:8: "But I say to you, make no oath at all, **either by heaven, for it is the throne of Yahweh.**"

Psalm 103:19 **Yahweh hath prepared his throne in the heavens;** and his kingdom ruleth overall.

Revelation 12:2 And immediately I was in the Spirit: and behold, **a throne was set in heaven, and one sat on the throne.**

Hebrews 1:14: "**Heaven is My throne** and the earth is My footstool."

A. THE THRONE ROOM:

Isaiah 6:1-3

1 In the year that king Uzziah died **I saw also Yahweh sitting upon a throne, high and lifted up, and his train filled the House.**

² **Above it stood the seraphims: each one had six wings; with twain he covered his face, and with twain he covered his feet, and with twain he did fly.**

³ And one cried unto another, and said, righteous, righteous, righteous, is Yahweh of hosts: the whole Earth is full of his righteousness.

Revelation 4:2-5

² And immediately I was in the Spirit: and behold, **a throne was set in heaven, and one sat on the throne.**

³ **And he that sat was to look upon like a jasper and a sardine stone: and there was a rainbow round about the throne, in sight like unto an emerald.**

⁴ **And round about the throne were four and twenty seats: and upon the seats I saw four and twenty elders sitting, clothed in white raiment; and they had on their head's crowns of gold.**

⁵ And out of the throne proceeded lightnings and thunderings and voices: and there were <u>seven lamps of fire burning before the throne</u>, which are the <u>seven Spirits of Yahweh</u>.

Isaiah 11:2

And the Spirit of Yahweh shall rest upon him, the Spirit of wisdom and understanding, the Spirit of counsel and might, the Spirit of knowledge and of the fear of Yahweh;

1. **Spirit of Yahweh**

2. **Spirit of Wisdom**

3. **Spirit of Understanding**

4. **Spirit of Counsel**

5. **Spirit of Strength**

6. **Spirit of Knowledge**

7. **Spirit of Fear, of Yahweh**

1 KING 22:19

And he said, Hear thou therefore the word of Yahweh: **I saw Yahweh sitting on his throne, and all the host of heaven standing by him on his right hand and on his left**

Revelation 5:6 Then I saw a Lamb, looking as if it had been slain, standing at the center of the throne, encircled by the four living creatures and the elders. <u>The Lamb had</u> seven horns and <u>seven eyes</u>, which are <u>the seven spirits of Yahweh sent out into all the Earth</u>.

Now you can see why Yahweh is the Messiah's name.

6 And <u>before the throne there was a sea of glass like unto crystal</u>: and in the midst of the throne, and round about the throne, were four beasts full of eyes before and behind.

Revelation 15:2

And I saw as it were a <u>sea of glass mingled with fire</u>: and <u>them that had gotten the victory over the beast, and over his image, and over his mark, and over the number of his name, stand on the sea of glass</u>, having the harps of Yahweh.

Revelation 15:2-5

2 And I saw as it were a sea of glass mingled with fire:<u> and them that had gotten the victory over the beast, and over his image, and over his mark, *and* over the number of his name, stand on the sea of glass, having the harps of Yahweh.</u>

3 And they sing the song of Moses the servant of Yahweh, and the song of the Lamb, saying, Great and marvelous *are* thy works, Yahweh; just and true *are* thy ways, thou King of believers.

4 Who shall not fear thee, O Yahweh, and honor thy name? for *thou* only *art* righteous: for all nations shall come and worship before thee; for thy judgments are made manifest.

5 And <u>out of the throne proceeded lightnings and thunderings and voices: and there were seven lamps of fire burning before the throne, they are reflecting off the</u>

floor which makes the floor look like it is mingled with fire, which they are standing on.

I will put these pieces of scripture together: <u>Seven lamps of fire burning before the throne; before the throne, there was a sea of glass like crystal</u>; as it were a <u>sea of glass mingled with fire; stand on the</u> sea of glass. This is the crystal-looking floor and the fire from the 7 lamps of fire reflecting off of it.

5 And <u>out of the throne proceeded lightnings and thunderings and voices: and there were seven lamps of fire burning before the throne, they are reflecting off the floor which makes the floor look like it is mingled with fire, which they are standing on.</u>

This should also show that His throne is on a mothership spacecraft that will sit its feet on the Mount of Olives. Zachariah 14:4 And his feet shall stand in that day upon the mount of Olives, which is before Zion on the East, and the mount of Olives shall cleave in the midst thereof toward the East and toward the west, and there shall be a very great valley, and half of the mountain shall remove toward the North and half of it toward the South.

Ezekiel 1:26-28

26 And above the firmament that was over their heads was the likeness of a throne, as the appearance of a sapphire stone: and upon the likeness of the throne was the likeness as the appearance of a man above upon it.

27 And I saw as the colour of amber, as the appearance of fire round about within it, from the appearance of his loins even upward, and from the appearance of his loins even downward, I saw as it were the appearance of fire, and it had brightness round about.

²⁸ As **the appearance of the bow that is in the cloud in the day of rain, so was the appearance of the brightness round about. This was the appearance of the likeness of the righteousness of Yahweh.** And when I saw it, I fell upon my face, and I heard a voice of one that spake.

Psalms 68:34 Ascribe ye strength unto Yahweh: his excellency is over Judaea, and **his strength is in the clouds.**

CHAPTER 13

PHILLIP TRANSPORTED

Act 8:39-40

39. And when they came up out of the water, the Spirit of Yahweh caught away Philip, that the eunuch saw him no more; and he went on his way rejoicing.

40. But Philip was found at Azotus: and passing through he taught in all the cities, till he came to Caesarea.

NOTE: Just like Eliyah, Phillip was taken up and taken somewhere else. A spacecraft did this, too. Yahweh the Father is Spirit, and he is the one that draws the people up into the spacecraft or spacecrafts.

CHAPTER 14

PAUL ON THE ROAD TO DAMASCUS

PAUL'S CONVERSION

Acts 9:3, 7

3. And as he journeyed, he came near Damascus: and **suddenly there shined round about him a light from heaven**:

7. And the men which journeyed with him stood speechless, **hearing a voice**, but seeing no man.

Acts 22:6-11

6. And it came to pass, that, as I made my journey, and came nigh unto Damascus about noon, **suddenly there shone from heaven a great light round about me.**

9. And <u>they that were with me saw indeed the light and</u> were afraid; but <u>they heard not the voice</u> of him that spake to me.

11. And **when I could not see for the brilliance of that light**, being led by the hand of them that were with me, I came into Damascus.

This was a spacecraft. It was about noon, and the light was even brighter than what the light of the sun was.

EXPLANATION OF REVELATION 1:14-15

14. His head and his hairs were white like wool, as white as snow; and his eyes were as a flame of fire;

15. And his feet like unto fine brass, as if they burned in a furnace; and his voice as the sound of many waters.

This is describing Yahweh Messiah in a spacecraft.

"His hairs were white like wool, as white as snow."

If you had a bright light shining on you, like what happened to Paul on the road to Damascus.

Your hair would look White no matter what color it was. **That powerful light came from a spacecraft.**

"**His eyes were as a flame of fire.**"

Psalms 104:3-4

3 He lays the beams of His upper chambers in the waters: He makes the clouds His chariot; He walks upon the wings of the wind;

4. He makes the winds His messengers, flaming fire His ministers.

(Spacecraft)

"His feet like unto fine brass, as if they burned in a furnace."

<u>Feet of fine brass is speaking of the feet of a spacecraft made like unto fine brass.</u>

Zechariah 14:4 And <u>his feet shall stand in that day upon the mount of Olives</u>, which *is* before Zion on the East, and the mount of Olives shall cleave in the midst thereof toward the East and toward the west, *and there shall be* a very great valley; and half of the mountain shall remove toward the North, and half of it toward the South.

<u>This is a mothership spacecraft.</u>

"The sound of his voice is like many waters" 'trumpet'

CHAPTER 15

JOHN OF REVELATION WAS TAKEN UP INTO A SPACECRAFT

Revelation 4:1 After this I looked, and behold, a door was opened in heaven: and **the first voice which I heard was as it were of a trumpet talking with me,** which said, **come up hither**, and I will shew thee things which must be hereafter.

John was taken up into a spacecraft. Just like Moses and Elijah will be after they are killed.

Exodus 19:9 And Yahweh said unto Moses, Lo, I come unto thee in a thick cloud, that the people may hear when I speak with thee and believe thee forever. And Moses told the words of the people unto Yahweh.

CHAPTER 16

SECOND GOG AND MAGOG WAR:

The judgment war that brings this Earth to its end. This happens after the Millennial Kingdom.

WW3 IS THE FIRST GOG AND MAGOG WAR

REVELATION 20: 7-9

7 And **when the thousand years are expired, Satan shall be loosed out of his prison,**

8 And shall **go out to deceive the nations which are in the four quarters of the Earth, Gog and Magog, to gather them together to battle:** the number of whom is as the sand of the sea.

9 And they went up on the breadth of the Earth, and compassed the camp of the Elect about, and the beloved city: **and fire came down from Yahweh out of heaven, and devoured them.**

FIRE COMES DOWN FROM A SPACECRAFT

Joel 2:4-11

<u>4</u> The appearance of them *is* as the appearance of horses; and as horsemen, so shall they run.

<u>5</u> Like the noise of chariots on the tops of mountains shall they leap, like the noise of a flame of fire that devoureth the stubble, as a strong people set in battle array.

6 Before their face the people shall be much pained: all faces shall gather blackness.

7 They shall run like mighty men; they shall climb the wall like men of war; and they shall march everyone on his ways, and they shall not break their ranks:

8 Neither shall one thrust another; they shall walk everyone in his path: and *when* they fall upon the sword, they shall not be wounded.

9 They shall run to and fro in the city; they shall run upon the wall; they shall climb up upon the houses; they shall enter in at the windows like a thief.

10 The Earth shall quake before them; the heavens shall tremble: the sun and the moon shall be dark, and the stars shall withdraw their shining:

11 And the Yahweh shall utter his voice before His army: for his camp *is* very great: for *he is* strong that executeth his word: for the day of Yahweh *is* great and very terrible; and who can abide it?

In verses 4 and 5, Joel is speaking of spacecraft and it's like Yahweh's Messengers went forth out of them like an army; whether they are on foot or riding some kind of machine is not plain.

Rev 19:11-15 – speaking of spacecraft at the time of the Armageddon War.

11. And I saw heaven opened and behold a white horse; and he that sat upon him was called Faithful and true, and in righteousness he doeth judge and make war.

12. His eyes were as a flame of fire, and on his head were many crowns; and he had a name written, that no man knew, but he himself.

13. And he was clothed with a vesture dipped in blood: and his name is called The Word of Yahweh.

14. And <u>the armies which were in heaven followed him upon the white horse,</u> clothed in fine lined, white and clean.

15. And out of his mouth goeth a sharp sword, that with it <u>he should smite the nations:</u> and <u>he shall rule the with a rod of iron;</u> and <u>he treadeth the winepress of the fierceness and wrath of the Almighty Yahweh.</u>

Joel 2:2,11

2. A day of darkness and gloom, a day of clouds and blackness. Like dawn spreading across the mountains a large and mighty army comes, such as never was in ancient times nor ever will be in ages to come.

11. Yahweh thunders at the head of his army; HIS FORCE IS BEYOND NUMBER; and mighty are those who obey His command. The day of Yahweh is great, it is dreadful. Who can endure it?

Note: Coming leading an enumerable army in spacecraft. There will be so many that they will actually block out the sun.

Psalm 68:17

17. <u>The Chariots of Yahweh are twenty thousand, even thousands of Messengers: Yahweh is among them, as in Sinai,</u> in the righteous place.

Isaiah 66:15-16

15. For, <u>Yahweh will come with fire, and with his chariots/spacecrafts like a whirlwind, to render his anger with fury, and his rebuke with flames of fire.</u>

16. For <u>by fire and by his sword will Yahweh plead with all flesh:</u> and <u>the slain of Yahweh shall be many</u>.

Zechariah 9:14

<u>Then Yahweh will appear over them; his arrow will flash like lightning. The Sovereign Yahweh will sound the trumpet; He will march in the storms of the South,</u>

NOTE: The horse representing a mode of transportation. Why would a horse be able to ride through space, but man must wear a spacesuit to survive? Why does other scriptures state He is coming again in clouds or chariots? These prove they represent a form of transportation.

By Christian standards, he will ride a horse through space, then jump on a cloud and descend the rest of the way when he reaches the Earth's atmosphere, with all his Messengers singing. Of course not. But Christians believe in Santa, Cupid, Easter bunnies, witches and goblins, and tooth fairies, so it was easy to convince them of this.

CHAPTER 17

INTO THE CATCHING-UP SPACECRAFT

FROM A CELESTIAL TO A TERRESTRIAL BODY, TO BE TAKEN UP INTO SPACECRAFT:

1 Corinthians 15: 40,44; 46-57

40 There are also celestial bodies, and bodies terrestrial: but the esteem of the celestial is one, and the righteousness of the terrestrial is another.

44 It is sown a natural body; it is raised a spiritual body. There is a natural body, and there is a spiritual body.

45 And so it is written, The first man Adam was made a living soul; the last Adam was made a quickening spirit.

46 Howbeit that was not first which is spiritual, but that which is natural; and afterward that which is spiritual.

47 The first man is of the earth, earthy; the second man is Yahweh from heaven.

48 As is the earthy, such are they also that are earthy: and as is the heavenly, such are they also that are heavenly.

49 And as we have borne the image of the earthy, we shall also bear the image of the heavenly.

50 Now this I say, brethren, that flesh and blood cannot inherit the kingdom of Yahweh; neither doth corruption inherit incorruption.

51 Behold, I shew you a mystery; We shall not all sleep, but we shall all be changed,

52 In a moment, in the twinkling of an eye, at the last trump: for the trumpet shall sound, and the dead shall be raised incorruptible, and we shall be changed.

53 For this corruptible must put on incorruption, and this mortal must put on immortality.

54 So when this corruptible shall have put on incorruption, and this mortal shall have put on immortality, then shall be brought to pass the saying that is written, Death is swallowed up in victory.

55 O death, where is thy sting? O grave, where is thy victory?

56 The sting of death is transgression; and the strength of transgression is the law.

57 But thanks be to Yahweh, which giveth us the victory through our Master Yahweh Messiah.

I BELIEVE WHEN A PERSON IS CHANGED INSTANTLY FROM A CELESTIAL TO A TERRESTRIAL BODY IT WILL GIVE A PERSON THE ABILITY TO BREATHE NO MATTER HOW HIGH THEY GO UP INTO THE ATMOSPHERE OF HEAVEN.

YAHWEH'S SPACECRAFT

Yahweh returns in spacecraft and all the wheat will be caught up into them,
The ones that are saved from Yahweh's wrath, those who had served Him.
Then Yahweh and His Messengers like birds flying, burns up all the chaff.
People never dreamed that all this will be done with Yahweh's spacecraft.

After this a great voice of many people in heaven and praising Yahweh,
for avenging the blood of His Elect, while the smoke ascended their way.
They are in spacecraft in heaven above the Earth, when this praise is done.
Then the Elect come right back to this Earth with Yahweh Messiah, the Son.

A POST-TRIBULATION NOT A PRETRIBULATION "CATCHING UP" - NO SUCH THING CALLED A "RAPTURE"

Matthew 24:29-31

29 **Immediately after the tribulation of those days** shall the sun be darkened, and the moon shall not give her light, and the stars shall fall from heaven, and the powers of the heavens shall be shaken: **STARS THAT FALL FROM HEAVEN I BELIEVE IS SATAN'S AND HIS MESSENGERS SPACECRAFT THAT WILL FIGHT YAHWEH AT HIS COMING.**

30 And **then shall appear the sign of the Son of man in heaven:** and then shall all the tribes of the Earth mourn, and they shall see the Son of man coming in the clouds of heaven with power and great righteousness.

31 And **he shall send his Messengers with a great sound of a trumpet, and they shall gather together his Elect from the four winds, from one end of heaven to the other.**

Mark 13:24, 26-27

24 But in those days, after that tribulation, the sun shall be darkened, and the moon shall not give her light,

26 And then shall they see the Son of man coming in the clouds with great power and righteousness.

27 And then shall he send his Messengers and shall gather together his elect from the four winds, from the uttermost part of the Earth to the uttermost part of heaven. <-- THIS WAS ADDED TO THE VERSE.

THE ARMAGEDDON WAR IS WHAT ENDS THE TRIBULATION PERIOD AND YAHWEH MESSIAH RETURNS DURING THAT TIME AND ENDS THE WAR AND TRIBULATION PERIOD AT HIS COMING AND THE TIMES OF THE GENTILES. ALL THE ABOVE PROVES HIS RETURN IS AT THE END OF THE TRIBULATION PERIOD.

Daniel 12:1-13

1 And at that time shall Michael stand up, the great prince which standeth for the children of thy people: and there shall be a time of trouble, such as never was since there was a nation even to that same time: and at that time thy people shall be delivered, every one that shall be found written in the book.

2 And many of them that sleep in the dust of the Earth shall awake, some to everlasting life, and some to shame and everlasting contempt.

3 And they that be wise shall shine as the brightness of the firmament; and they that turn many to righteousness as the stars for ever and ever.

4 But thou, O Daniel, **shut up the words, and seal the book, even to the time of the end: many shall run to and fro, and knowledge shall be increased.**

5 Then I Daniel looked, and behold, there stood other two, the one on this side of the bank of the river, and the other on that side of the bank of the river.

⁶ And one said to the man clothed in linen, which was upon the waters of the river, how long shall it be to the end of these wonders?

⁷ And I heard the man clothed in linen, which was upon the waters of the river, when he held up his right hand and his left hand unto heaven, and sware by him that liveth forever that **it shall be for a time, times, and a half; and when he shall have accomplished to scatter the power of the righteous people, all these things shall be finished.**

⁸ And I heard, but I understood not: then said I, O my Master, **what shall be the end of these things?**

⁹ And he said, go thy way, Daniel: for **the words are closed and sealed till the time of the end.**

¹⁰ Many shall be purified, and made white, and tried; but the wicked shall do wickedly: and none of the wicked shall understand; but the wise shall understand.

¹¹ And from the time that the daily offering shall be taken away, and the abomination that maketh desolate set up, there shall be a thousand two hundred and ninety days.

¹² Blessed is he that waiteth, and cometh to the thousand three hundred and five and thirty days.

¹³ But go thou thy way till the end be: for thou shalt rest and stand in thy lot at the end of the days.

1 Thessalonians 4:17

17. Then we which are alive and remain shall be **(caught up together with them IN THE CLOUDS,) to meet Yahweh in the air**; and **so, shall we ever be with Yahweh.**

Here again it says IN, not ON the Clouds.

John 14:3

3. And if I go and prepare a place for you, I will come again and receive you to myself; that where I am, there you may be also.

NOTE: If Yahweh is reigning on this Earth then no one can be in heaven.

Matthew 24:29

Immediately after the tribulation of those days shall the sun be darkened, and the moon shall not give her light, and the STARS shall fall from heaven, and the powers of the heavens shall be shaken: NOTE: There is going to be so many spacecraft when Yahweh comes that they will block the light from the sun and moon. Spacecraft in scriptures are spoken of as the Star or stars, a cloud or clouds, chariots, chariots of fire, white horse, horses, even Cherub. If a spacecraft just sits still in the heavens, you could not tell it apart from a literal star. I remember they announced on the news that at a certain time at night, you would be able to see the space station. I watched the night sky where they said it would be and I seen it, it looked just like a shining star, except it was moving at a steady pace across the night skies, right over the House, not like a shooting star.

Just like the Star of Bethlehem was a spacecraft, it was not a literal star. This Star led them right to the House where Immanuel was living; when the Wisemen saw what it really was, they worshiped it.

Matthew 24:30-31

30. And then shall appear the sign of the Son of man in heaven: and then shall all the tribes of the Earth mourn, and they shall see the Son of man coming in the CLOUDS of heaven with power and great esteem.

NOTE: Once again, Clouds are Spacecraft.

31. And he shall send his Messengers with a great sound of a trumpet, and they shall gather together his Elect from the four winds, from one end of heaven to the other.

Mark 13:26-27

26. And <u>then shall they see the Son of man coming in the CLOUDS</u> with great power and esteem.

27. And <u>then shall He send His Messengers and shall gather together his Elect from the four winds,</u> <u>from the uttermost part of the Earth to the uttermost; part of heaven.</u>

Revelation 1:7

7. <u>Behold, he cometh with clouds;</u> and <u>every eye shall see him</u>, and they also which pieced him: an all kindreds of the Earth shall wail because of him,

COMING IN SPACECRAFT

1 Thessalonians 4:16-18

16. <u>For Yahweh himself shall descend from heaven with a shout,</u> <u>with the voice of the Archmessenger, and with the trump of Yahweh</u> and <u>the dead in Yahweh shall rise first:</u>

17. Then <u>we which are alive and remain shall be (caught up together with them in the clouds,)</u> <u>to meet Yahweh in the air;</u> and <u>so, shall we ever be with Yahweh.</u>

IN SPACECRAFT

<u>Why are they caught up in the clouds to meet Yahweh in the air? Why not just meet him in the air without the clouds?</u> Because the CLOUDS are spacecraft, and the Spirit of Yahweh will draw people up into them to meet Yahweh in the air, he knows which ones are his by the **Spirit that is within them. That's why the Elect will be changed in the twinkling of an eye from an earthly body to a terrestrial body.**

I also believe that people will all be 30 years old on the New Earth, the prime age of life. This is how old Immanuel was when he started his teaching Ministery in Galilee.

Mark 16:5 And entering into the sepulcher, **they saw a young man** sitting on the right side, clothed in a long white garment; and they were affrighted.

This Messenger was a young man. If people never get old on the New Earth I think 30 is a perfect age to stay.

CHAPTER 18

PART 1 NEW ZION

Revelation 21:1-5

¹ And **I saw a new heaven and a new earth:** for **the first heaven and the first Earth were passed away;** and there was no more sea.

² **And I John saw the righteous city, new Zion, coming down from Yahweh out of heaven, prepared as a bride adorned for her husband.** I believe there are one of three ways that New Zion could come down on the new Earth.

Revelation 3:12 Him that overcometh will I make a pillar in the House of my Father, and he shall go no more out: and I will write upon him the name of my Father, and the name of the city of my Father, which is new Zion, which cometh down out of heaven from my Father: and I will write upon him my new name.

Revelation 19:7-9

⁷ Let us be glad and rejoice and **give honor to him: for the marriage of the Lamb is come, and his wife hath made herself ready.**

⁸ And **to her was granted that she should be arrayed in fine linen, clean and white: for the fine linen is the righteousness of the Elect.**

⁹ And he saith unto me, Write, **Blessed *are* they which are called unto the marriage supper of the Lamb.** And he saith unto me, **these are the true sayings of Yahweh.**

Galatians 4:26

²⁶ But **NEW ZION which is above is free, which is the mother of us all**.

Isaiah 65:

18 But **be ye glad and rejoice forever *in that* which I create: for, behold, I create Zion a rejoicing, and her people a joy.**

19 And **I will rejoice in Zion, and joy in my people: and the voice of weeping shall be no more heard in her, nor the voice of crying.**

John 14:2-5 In my Father's House are many mansions: if it were not so, I would have told you. I go to prepare a place for you.

Revelation 3:12 Him that overcometh will I make a pillar in the House of my Father, and he shall go no more out: and I will write upon him the name of my Father, and the name of the city of my Father, which is new Zion, which cometh down out of heaven from my Father: and I will write upon him my new name.

3 And I heard a great voice out of heaven saying, Behold, **Yahweh *is* with men, and he will dwell with them, and they shall be his people, and Yahweh himself shall be with them, *and be* their Father.**

4 And **Yahweh shall wipe away all tears from their eyes; and there shall be no more death, neither sorrow, nor crying, neither shall there be any more pain: for the former things are passed away.**

5 And **he that sat upon the throne** said, Behold, **I make all things new.** And he said unto me, write: **for these words are true and faithful.**

Revelation 21:9-19

9 And there came unto me one of the seven Messengers which had the seven vials full of the seven last plagues, and talked with me, saying, come hither, **I will shew thee the bride, the Lamb's wife.**

10 And **he carried me away in the Spirit to a great and high mountain, and shewed me that great city, the righteous Zion, descending out of heaven from Yahweh,**

THE DESCRIPTION OF THE CITY, NEW ZION. VERSES 11-27

11 Having the righteousness of Yahweh: and her light *was* like unto a stone most precious, even like a jasper stone, clear as crystal;

12 And had a wall great and high, *and* had twelve gates, and at the gates twelve Messengers, and names written thereon, which are *the names* of the twelve tribes of the children of Judaea:

13 On the east three gates; on the north three gates; on the south three gates; and on the west three gates.

14 And the wall of the city had twelve foundations, and in them the names of the twelve apostles of the Lamb.

15 And he that talked with me had a golden reed to measure the city, and the gates thereof, and the wall thereof.

16 And the city lieth foursquare, and the length is as large as the breadth: and he measured the city with the reed, twelve thousand furlongs. The length and the breadth and the height of it are equal.

17 And he measured the wall thereof, an hundred *and* forty *and* four cubits, ***according to*** **the measure of a man, that is, of the Messenger.**

IN IT'S DEMENTIONS IT WILL LOOK LIKE A SQUARE CUBE.

18 And the building of the wall of it was of jasper: and the city was pure gold, like unto clear glass.

19 And the foundations of the wall of the city were garnished with all manner of precious stones. The first foundation was jasper; the second, sapphire; the third, a chalcedony; the fourth, an emerald;

20 The fifth, sardonyx; the sixth, sardius; the seventh, chrysolite; the eighth, beryl; the ninth, a topaz; the tenth, a chrysoprasus; the eleventh, a jacinth; the twelfth, an amethyst.

21 And the twelve gates were twelve pearls; every several gate was of one pearl: and the street of the city was pure gold, as it were transparent glass.

22 And I saw no House [of Yahweh] therein: for Yahweh and the Lamb are the House of it.

23 And the city had no need of the sun, neither of the moon, to shine in it: for the righteousness of Yahweh did lighten it, and the Lamb *is* the light thereof.

24 And the nations of them which are redeemed shall walk in the light of it: and the kings of the Earth do bring their righteousness and honor into it.

25 And the gates of it shall not be shut at all by day: for there shall be no night there.

26 And they shall bring the righteousness and honor of the nations into it.

27 And there shall in no wise enter into it any thing that defileth, neither whatsoever worketh abomination, or maketh a lie: but they which are written in the Lamb's book of life.

Hebrews 12:22 But ye are come unto Mount Zion, and unto the city of the living Yahweh, the heavenly Zion, and to an innumerable company of Messengers,

CHAPTER 19

ELIJAH – ELISHA

2 Kings 2:11-12

¹¹ **And it came to pass, as they still went on, and talked, that,** behold, there appeared a chariot of fire, and horses of fire, and parted them both asunder; and Elijah went up by a whirlwind into heaven.

¹² **And** Elisha saw it, and he cried, My father, my father, the chariot of YAHWEH and the horsemen thereof. And he saw him no more: **and he took hold of his own clothes and rent them in two pieces.**

Isaiah 35:10

10. And the ransomed of Yahweh shall return and come to Zion with songs and everlasting joy upon their heads: they shall obtain joy and gladness, and sorrow and sighing shall flee away.

AS YOU CAN SEE THEY DID NOT GO TO HEAVEN, THEY CAME RIGHT BACK DOWN TO THIS EARTH FOR YAHWEH'S MILLENNIAL KINGDOM.

Revelation 5:11

11. And I beheld, and I heard the voice of many Messengers round about the throne and the beasts and the elders: and the number of them was ten thousand times ten thousand, and thousands of thousands.

NOTE: Ten thousand times ten thousand is one hundred million, but there are thousands of thousands more, they are enumerable.

Hebrews 12:22

22. But **ye come unto mount Zion, and unto the city of the living Yahweh, the heavenly Zion, <u>and to an innumerable company of Messengers.</u>**

CHAPTER 20

JUDAEA FLEEING EGYPT

THE MANNA RAINED DOWN FROM HEAVEN FOR THEIR 40 YEARS IN THE WILDERNESS <u>CAME FROM SPACECRAFT</u>, THE FOOD OF HIS MESSENGERS. Exodus 16:3,4,13,143. And the children of Judaea said to them, "We wish that we had died by the hand of Yahweh in the land of Egypt, when we sat by the meat pots, when we ate our fill of bread, for you have brought us out into this wilderness, to kill this whole assembly with hunger.

4. Then said Yahweh to Moses, "Behold, I will rain bread from the sky for you, and the people shall go out and gather a day's portion every day, that I may test them, whether they will walk in my law, or not.

13. And it came to pass, that at even the quails came up, and covered the camp: and in the morning the dew lay round about the host.

14. And when the dew that lay was gone up, behold, upon the face of the wilderness there lay a small round thing, as small as the hoar frost on the ground.

15. And when the children of Judaea saw it, they said one to another, It is manna: for they wist not what it was. And Moses said unto them, This is the bread which Yahweh hath given you to eat.

16. This is the thing which Yahweh hath commanded, Gather of it every man according to his eating, an omer for every man, according to the number of your persons; take ye every man for them which are in his tents.

17. And the children of Judaea did so, and gathered, some more, some less.

18. And when they did mete it with an omer, he that gathered much had nothing over, and he that gathered little had no lack; they gathered every man according to his eating.

People need to learn how to study instead of listening to lies that the world wants them to believe. Especially people who have no clue what scriptures teach because they are too busy trying to disprove them than to believe in them; enough truth has been left in them for anyone that will take the time to do some deep studies will find it.

A. MOSES ON MOUNT SINAI

Exodus 19:9 And Yahweh said unto Moses, Lo, I come unto thee in a thick cloud, that the people may hear when I speak with thee and believe thee forever. And Moses told the words of the people unto Yahweh.

Exodus 19:18-19

¹⁸ And mount Sinai was altogether on a smoke, because Yahweh descended upon it in fire: and the smoke thereof ascended as the smoke of a furnace, and the whole mount quaked, greatly.

IN A SPACECRAFT

¹⁹ And when the voice of the trumpet sounded long, and waxed louder and louder, Moses spake, and Yahweh answered him by a voice.

Isaiah 19:11

The burden of Egypt. Behold, **Yahweh rideth upon a swift cloud, and shall come into Egypt: and the idols of Egypt shall be moved at his presence, and the heart of Egypt shall melt in the midst of it.**

Exodus 19:9 And Yahweh said unto Moses, Lo, **I come unto thee in a thick cloud, that the people may hear when I speak with thee and** believe thee forever. And Moses told the words of the people unto Yahweh.

Exodus 13:21-22

21. And **Yahweh went before them by day in a pillar of a CLOUD, to lead them the way; and by night in a pillar of fire, to give them light; to go by day and night.**

By night _By day

22. **He took not away the pillar of the CLOUD by day, nor the pillar of fire by night,** from before the people.

This was a spacecraft.

Exodus 14:14

14. **Yahweh shall fight for you, and ye shall hold your peace.**

B. CROSSING THE RED SEA

The Red Sea runs South, and the wind comes from the East; this was done by spacecraft all night long and it dried up the land underneath the sea for them to crossover.

Exodus 14:22

22. and the **Judaeans went through the sea on dry ground, WITH A WALL OF WATER ON THEIR RIGHT HAND AND ON THE LEFT.**

NOTE: This is interesting here because there was a wall of water on both sides. Now, the Red Sea runs south, so any water on the North side would form a wall of water since the water keeps running toward the South. The water on the South side would keep moving South, so there could be no wall. So, it was at a place where the Red Sea emptied into another body of water, where it would push water back North to form another wall of water on the South side.

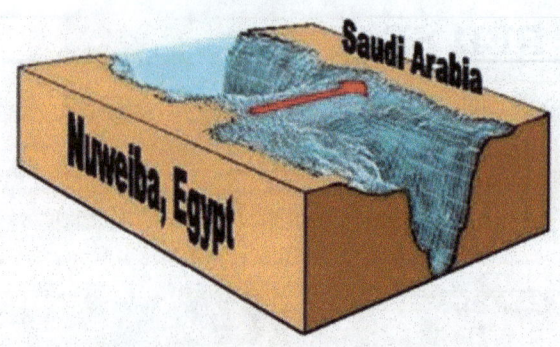

NOTICE: **Moses stretched out his hand over the sea, then it says a strong east wind all that night, dried the land and waters were divided. (IT WAS SPACECRAFT THAT DID IT)**

The distance across the Red Sea at this spot is a little over 8 miles. The land bridge is very wide, about 7-tenths of a mile wide, and is very flat in general. The sea bed is covered by sand and gravel, excellent for walking across.

So, as you should be able to figure out, there was no problem moving even 3 million people across at night. It was about a mile wide where they crossed. They had all night to cross the 8 miles, which an average person can walk a mile in about 20 minutes. Three square miles would hold 2,323,200 people--very close to the number of people crossing. So if they were 3 miles long or even more with animals and other things. So it would only have taken 3 or 4 hours to do the crossing. So they had plenty of time. Yahweh timed it right so the Egyptians would be crossing when the final ones got across. So He could drown all of the Egyptian army.

Exodus 14:8,10, 27

8. And with the blast of thy nostrils the waters were gathered together, the floods stood upright as a heap, and the depths were congealed in the heart of the sea.

10. **Thou didst blow with thy wind, the sea covered them: they sank as lead in the mighty waters.**

NOTE: This was done by the spacecraft, done by Yahweh.

27. And Moses stretched forth his hand over the sea, and the sea returned to his strength when the morning appeared; and the Egyptians fled against it; and Yahweh overthrew the Egyptians in the midst of the sea.

NOTICE: Moses stretched forth his hand over the sea, and the sea returned to its strength, WHEN MORNING APPEARED. **They crossed the Red Sea at night, not during the day.**

NOTICE TOO: That a spacecraft moved from in front of the Judaean camp to behind it, between the Egyptian camp and Judaean's camp. There was light to the Judaeans and darkness to the Egyptians. So they would not come near to each other. Judaea escaped at night.

Exodus 14:19-20

19. And **the Messenger of Yahweh, which went before the camp of Judaea, removed and went behind them; and the pillar of the CLOUD went from before their face, and stood behind them.**

20. And it came between the camp of the Egyptians and the camp of Judaea; and it was a cloud and darkness to them, but it gave light by night to these; so that the one came not near the other.

Exodus 16:10

And it came to pass, as Aaron spake unto the whole congregation of the children of Judaea, that they looked toward the wilderness, and behold, the glory/**spacecraft** of Yahweh appeared in the cloud.

Psalm 68:34

34. Ascribe ye strength unto the Yahweh: his excellency is over Judaea, **and his strength in the CLOUDS.**

Daniel 7:13

13. **I saw in the night visions, and behold, one like the Son of man came with the CLOUDS of heaven, and came to the Ancient of days, and they brought him near before him.**

Deuteronomy 31:15

15. And Yahweh appeared in the House in a PILLAR of a CLOUD: the PILLAR of the CLOUD stood over the door of the House.

Numbers 12:5,10

5. And **Yahweh came down in the PILLAR of the CLOUD, and stood in the door of the House, and called Aaron and Miriam**: and they both came.

10. And the CLOUD departed from off the House; and behold, Miriam became leprous, white as snow: and Aaron looked upon Miriam, and, behold, she was leprous.

Exodus 19:9,11,16

9. And Yahweh said unto Moses, Lo, I come unto thee in a THICK CLOUD, that the people may hear when I speak with thee and believe thee forever. And Moses told the words of the people unto Yahweh.

11. And be ready against the third day: for the third day Yahweh will come down in the sight of all the people upon mount Sinai. (In Spacecraft)

16. And it came to pass on the third day in the morning, that there were thunders and lightnings, and A THICK CLOUD UPON THE MOUNT, and the voice of the trumpet exceeding loud; so that all the people that *was* **in the camp trembled. 18. And mount Sinai was altogether on a smoke, because Yahweh descended upon it in fire: and the smoke thereof ascended as the smoke of a furnace, and the whole mount quaked greatly. (A Spacecraft did this.)**

Exodus 24:15,18

15. And Moses went up into the mount, and a CLOUD covered the mount.

18. And MOSES WENT INTO THE MIDST OF THE CLOUD, and gat him up into the mount: and Moses was in the mount forty days and forty nights.

Exodus 33:9-10,20-23

9. And it came to pass, as Moses entered into the tabernacle, the CLOUDY PILLAR descended, and stood at the door of the tabernacle, and Yahweh talked with Moses.

10. And all the people saw the CLOUDY PILLAR stand at the tabernacle door: and all the people rose up and worshiped, every man at his door.

20. And he said, thou canst not see my face: for there shall no man see me, and live.

21. And Yahweh said, Behold, there is a place by me, and thou shalt stand upon a rock.

22. And it shall come to pass, while my esteem passeth by, that I will put thee in a clift of the rock, and will cover thee with my hand while I pass by.

23. And I will take away mine hand, and thou shalt see my back parts: but my face shall not be seen.

This is Yahweh speaking from a spacecraft. The shape of the spacecraft was a pillar hiding in a cloud.

Let's go back to Matthew 17:5

5. While he yet spake, behold, a bright CLOUD overshadowed them: and behold a voice out of the CLOUD, which said, this is my beloved Son, in whom I am well pleased, hear ye him.

Psalm 80:1

1 Give ear, O Shepherd of Judaea, thou that leadest Joseph like a flock; **thou that dwellest between the cherubims, shine forth.**

Matthew 26:64

64. Immanuel saith unto him, thou hast said: nevertheless, I say unto you, Hereafter shall ye see the Son of man sitting on the right hand of power and coming in the CLOUDS of heaven.

Mark 14:62 And Immanuel said, I am; and you shall see the son of man sitting at the right hand of power and coming with the CLOUDS of heaven.

Exodus 40:34-38

34. Then a CLOUD covered the tent of the congregation, and the esteem of Yahweh filled the tabernacle.

35. And Moses was not able to enter into the tent of the congregation, because the cloud abode thereon, and the esteem of Yahweh filled the tabernacle.

36. And when the cloud was taken up from over the tabernacle, the children of Judaea went onward in all their journeys:

37. But if the CLOUD were not taken up, then they journeyed not till the day that it was taken up.

38. For the CLOUD of Yahweh was upon the Tabernacle by day, and fire was on it by night, in the sight of all the House of Judaea, throughout all their journeys.

The cloud again being a spacecraft.

Exodus 34:5-6

5. Then **Yahweh descended in the CLOUD, and stood with him there, and proclaimed the Name of YAHWEH.**

Exodus 16:10

6. **Yahweh passed in front of him, and proclaimed: YAHWEH, YAHWEH, merciful and compassionate, longsuffering, and abounding in righteousness and truth**.

Again, the cloud is a spacecraft.

Numbers 11:16,17

16. And Yahweh said unto Moses, Gather unto me seventy men of the elders of Judaea, whom thou knowest to be the elders of the people, and officers over them; and bring them unto the House of the assembly, that they may stand there with thee.

17. And I will come down and talk with thee there: and I will take of the Spirit which is upon thee, and will put it upon them; and they shall bear the burden of the people with thee, that thou bear it not thyself alone.

C. CROSSING THE JORDON RIVER

¹³ The priests who carry the ark of Yahweh, Yahweh of the whole Earth, will stand in the water of the Jordan. Then the water flowing from upstream will stop and stand up like a dam."

THIS WAS DONE WITH A SPACECRAFT

¹⁴ So they broke camp to cross the Jordan River. The priests who carried the ark of the promise went ahead of the people.

¹⁵ (The Jordan overflows all its banks during the harvest season.)[a] When the priests who were carrying the ark came to the edge of the Jordan River and set foot in

¹⁶ the water, the water stopped flowing from upstream. The water rose up like a dam as far away as the city of Adam near Zarethan. The water flowing down toward the Sea of the Plains (the Dead Sea) was completely cut off. Then **the people crossed from the east side L of the Jordan River directly opposite Jericho.**

17 The priests who carried the ark of Yahweh's promise stood firmly on dry ground in the middle of the Jordan until the whole nation of Judaea had crossed the Jordan River on dry ground.

CHAPTER 21

ELISHA AND THE CHARIOTS OF FIRE

Numbers 11:25

25. And **Yahweh came down in a cloud, and spake unto him, and took of the spirit that *was* upon him, and gave *it* unto the seventy elders: and it came to pass, *that*, when the spirit rested upon them, they prophesied, and did not cease.**

Chariot / Mothership with smaller spacecraft / horses

Jeremiah 4:13

13. **Behold, he shall come up as CLOUDS, and his CHARIOTS shall be as a whirlwind: his HORSES are swifter than eagles.** Woe unto us! for we are spoiled.

2 Kings 6:8, 14-18

8. Then the king of Syria warred against Judaea, and took counsel with his servants, saying, In such and such a place shall be my camp.

14. **Therefore, sent he thither horses, and chariots, and a great host: and they came by night, and compassed the city about.**

15. **And when the servant of the man of Yahweh was risen, and gone forth, behold, a host compassed the city both with horses and chariots**. And his servant said unto him, Alas, my master: how shall we do?

16. And he answers, Fear not; for they that be with us are more than they that be with them.

17. And Elisha prayed, and said Yahweh, pray thee, open his eyes, that he may see. And **Yahweh opened the eyes of the young man; and he saw: and behold, the mountain was full of horses and chariots of fire round about Elisha.**

Horses and Chariots of fire are spacecraft and notice they can be unseen and be before your eyes.

CHAPTER 22

ELIJAH TAKEN UP IN A CHARIOT OF FIRE

2 Kings 2: 10,11,12

10. And he said, thou hast asked a hard thing: nevertheless, if thou see me when I am taken from thee, it shall be so unto thee; but if not, it shall not be so.

11. And it came to pass, as they still went on, and talked, that, behold, **there appeared a chariot of fire, and horses of fire, and parted them both asunder; and Elijah went up by a whirlwind into heaven.**

Chariots of fire are spacecraft. The horses are the smaller spacecraft that comes from the bigger one called a Chariot.

12. And Elisha saw it, and he cried, My father, my father, **the chariot of Judaea, and the horsemen thereof.** And he saw him no more: and he took hold of his own clothes and rent them in two pieces.

COMPARE JEREMIAH 4:13 WITH THE 3 VERSES ABOVE.

Jeremiah 4:13

13. Behold, **he shall come up as CLOUDS, and his CHARIOTS shall be as a whirlwind: his HORSES are swifter than eagles. Woe unto us! for we are spoiled.**

Ezekiel 1:4-14 describes the same as in Ezekiel chapter 10

Ezekiel 1:4-14

4 And **I looked, and behold, a whirlwind came out of the north, a great cloud, and a fire infolding itself, and a brightness was about it, and out of the midst thereof as the colour of amber, out of the midst of the fire.**

5 **Also out of the midst thereof came the likeness of four living creatures. And this was their appearance; they had the likeness of a man.**

6 And **everyone had four faces, and everyone had four wings**.

7 **And their feet were straight feet; and the sole of their feet was like the sole of a calf's foot: and they sparkled like the color of burnished brass.**

8 **And they had the hands of a man under their wings on their four sides; and they four had their faces and their wings.**

9 **Their wings were joined one to another; they turned not when they went; they went every one straight forward.**

Ezekiel 1:10-14

10 **As for the likeness of their faces, they four had the face of a man, and the face of a lion, on the right side: and they four had the face of an ox on the left side; they four also had the face of an eagle.**

11 **Thus were their faces: and their wings were stretched upward; two wings of every one were joined one to another, and two covered their bodies.**

12 And **they went every one straight forward: whither the spirit was to go, they went; and they turned not when they went**

13 As **for the likeness of the living creatures, their appearance was like burning coals of fire, and like the appearance of lamps: it went up and down among the living creatures; and the fire was bright, and out of the fire went forth lightning.**

14 And **the living creatures ran and returned as the appearance of a flash of lightning.**

Ezekiel 10:19-21Exodus 19:18-19

19 And **when the living creatures went, the wheels went by them: and when the living creatures were lifted up from the earth, the wheels were lifted up.**

20 **Whithersoever the spirit was to go, they went, thither was their spirit to go; and the wheels were lifted up over against them: for the spirit of the living creature was in the wheels.**

21 **When those went, these went; and when those stood, these stood; and when those were lifted up from the earth, the wheels were lifted up over against them: for the spirit of the living creature was in the wheels.**

CHAPTER 23
RONALD REAGAN AND ALIENS SPEECH

Ronald Reagan was the first President of the United States to talk about the possibility of an alien invasion from outer space, and he has done so in three different speeches. Ronald Reagan stated to the United Nations that the world had to come together in case we are attacked by aliens from another world.December 4th, 1985:

While addressing a group of high school students in Fallston, Maryland..." I couldn't help but say to Gorbachev, just think how easy his task and mine might be...if suddenly there was a threat to this world from some other species from another planet outside in the universe. We'd forget all the little local differences .... between our countries....and find out once and for all that we really are all human."

September 21, 1987:

Before the United Nations General Assembly: " In our obsession with antagonisms of the moment," said Reagan, "we often forget how much unites all the members of humanity. Perhaps we need some outside, universal threat to make us recognize this common bond. I occasionally think about how quickly our differences worldwide would vanish if we were facing an alien threat from outside this world. And yet, I ask you," he went on, "is not an alien threat already among us? What could be more alien to the universal aspirations of our peoples than war and the threat of war?"

This is what the government wants you to believe they look like when they look just like us. THERE WILL BE NO SUCH THING CALLED AN ALIEN ABDUCTION.

The first thing Yahweh did in Creation was to make flesh for himself so he could dwell among men. Then he created the Messengers in his image, then he created man after his image and why we look like them, and they look like us in human form. The very reason that scriptures state that we could entertain Messengers unaware, they do not have wings like pictures in Christianity propose. There is no such thing as the Aliens that the government wants you to believe exists. Yahweh and the Messengers were on this earth before man was even created.

May 5th, 1988:

As President Reagan leaves the White House on the way to Chicago. Talking about the importance of frankness, for a desire for peaceful solutions and wars, he goes on to say..."But I've often wondered what if all of us in the world discovered that we were threatened by an outer--a power from another planet." Reagan said. "Wouldn't we all of a sudden find that we didn't have any differences between us at all? We were all human beings, citizens of the world and wouldn't we come together to fight that particular threat?" The president said.

This is what the government wants you to believe they look like when they look just like us.

When armies of every nation go against Zion, Satan, and his messengers will be there too to fight Yahweh at his coming. So, this attack from another world will actually be when Yahweh returns. I believe Satan will tell this world he will help protect us with his spacecraft.

Yahweh will kill Satan at this time, and he will be dead for 1000 years. Then Yahweh will loose him one last time to deceive the world after Yahweh himself has taught the people, so there will be no more excuses. When the end comes, that will be the final judgment of this world. I don't believe that Yahweh would let his spacecrafts be seen by man until he is ready to reveal them at His coming when he wipes out the armies. I believe this is going to be one magnificent scene when it comes to then pass.

http://www.youtube.com/watch?v=F5ncXJJIw60

Don't you know the people had to have made fun of Noah and his ark until the rains came, then you know they would have wanted in.

Now, you can make fun of me for what I know, just like Noah. When it all comes down, then you also will wish you would have listened.

Winston Churchill was accused of ordering a cover-up of a Second World War encounter between a UFO and an RAF bomber because he feared public "panic" and loss of faith in religion, newly released secret files.

During their flight on the English coast, possibly near Cumbria, their aircraft was approached by a metallic UFO which shadowed them.

Photographs of the object, which the crew claimed had "hovered noiselessly" near the plane, were taken by the crew. The existence of spacecraft has been hidden within Christianity, another thing to deceive people about. Scriptures prove Yahweh is coming back in spacecraft.

I believe it was in 1950 that a spacecraft was seen over Louisville, Kentucky, and they tracked it over Bowling Green and then to Franklin, Kentucky, Where I used to live, in both places, when an Air Force Pilot caught up with it, he came up beside it, then he reported with his last words, "My god there are humans in that thing," then the plane crashed in Simpson county outside of Franklin, killing the pilot. You can google it for the full story.

NASA: Huge UFO fleet is behind the Moon – intentions

http://mostreadnews.uk/template-explore/k2/categories/487-nasa-huge-ufo-fleet-is-behind-the-moon-intentions-unknown

CHAPTER 24

ARMAGEDDON WAR – YAHWEH USES SPACECRAFT

REVELATION 1:7 Behold he comes with the clouds; and every eye will see him, and they that pierced him; and all the tribes of the earth

ISAIAH 66:15 For , Behold, Yahweh will come with fire, and his chariots shall be like the whirlwind; to render his anger with fierceness, and his rebuke with flames of fire of fire.

16 For by fire will Yahweh execute judgement, and his sword, upon all flesh; and the killed of Yahweh shall be many.

Isaiah 31:5 "As birds flying, so will Yahweh of hosts defend Zion; defending also he will deliver *it; and* passing over he will preserve it."

MILLENNIAL KINGDOM AFTER ARMAGEDDON WAR:

ZECHARIAH 14:4 And his feet shall stand in that day upon the mount of Olives, which *is* before Zion on the east, and the mount of Olives shall cleave in the midst thereof toward the east and toward the west, *and there shall be* a very great valley; and half of the mountain shall remove toward the north, and half of it toward the south.

A mothership with his throne on it will do this when he sets up his Millennial Kingdom here on this earth.

Micah 1:3

Look! Yahweh is coming from His dwelling place; He comes down and treads the high places of the earth.

Note: In a mothership spacecraft.

Isaiah 42:13

13. Yahweh shall go forth as a mighty man, he shall stir up jealousy like a man of war: he shall cry, yea, roar; he shall prevail against his enemies.

14. I have long time holden my peace; I have been still and refrained myself: now will I cry like a travailing woman; I will destroy and devour at once.

15. I will make waste mountains and hills and dry up all their herbs; and I will make the rivers islands, and I will dry up the pools.

Isaiah 31:4-8

4. Yahweh Almighty will come down to do battle on Mount Zion and on its heights.

5. As birds flying, **(SPACECRAFT)** Yahweh of hosts will defend Zion; defending also He will deliver it; and passing over He will preserve it.

6. Return to him you have so greatly revolted against, O Judaeans.

7. For in that day every one of you will reject the idols of silver and gold your transgressing hands have made.

8. "Assyria will fall by a sword that is not of man; a sword, not of mortals, will devour them.

Joel 2:2-6

Blow ye the trumpet in Zion, and sound an alarm in my righteous mountain: let all the inhabitants of the land tremble: for the day of Yahweh cometh, for *it is* nigh at hand;

2. A day of darkness and of gloominess, a day of clouds and of thick darkness, as the morning spread upon the mountains: a great people and a strong; there hath not been ever the like, neither shall be any more after it, *even* to the years of many generations.

3. A fire devoureth before them; and behind them a flame burneth: the land *is* as the garden of Eden before them, and behind them a desolate wilderness; yea, and nothing shall escape them.

THERE ARE GOING TO BE SO MANY SPACECRAFTS ON THE DAY OF YAHWEH THAT THEY WILL BLOCK THE LIGHT OF THE SUN, MOON, AND STARS.

Isaiah 13:9-13

9Behold, the day of Yahweh cometh, cruel both with wrath and fierce anger, to lay the land desolate: and he shall destroy the transgressors thereof out of **it.**

10 For the stars of heaven and the constellations thereof shall not give their light: the sun shall be darkened in his going forth, and the moon shall not cause her light to shine.

11 And I will punish the world for *their* evil, and the wicked for their iniquity; and I will cause the arrogancy of the proud to cease, and will lay low the haughtiness of the terrible.

12 I will make a man more precious than fine gold; even a man than the golden wedge of Ophir.

13Therefore **I will shake the heavens, and the earth shall remove out of her place, in the wrath of Yahweh of hosts, and in the day of his fierce anger.**

THIS WORLD IS IN BIG TROUBLE WHEN YAHWEH POURS OUT HIS WRATH UPON IT.

CHAPTER 25
THEY HAVE BEEN HID FROM THE NEWER GENERATIONS:

Paintings with UFOs. Most likely done in the 11th to 13th centuries in the time of the Crusades and Monarchy.

NASA: Huge UFO fleet is behind the Moon – intentions-unknown

http://mostreadnews.uk/template-explore/k2/categories/487-nasa-huge-ufo-fleet-is-behind-the-moon-intentions-unknown

CHAPTER 26

VERSES OF DECEIT:

During times of universal deceit, speaking the truth becomes a revolutionary act. ---George Orwell

Proverbs 20:17 - Bread of deceit is sweet to a man; but afterwards his mouth shall be filled with gravel.

Proverbs 26:24-26 - He that hateth dissembleth with his lips, and layeth up deceit within him;

Psalms 120:2 - Deliver my soul, Yahweh, from lying lips, and from a deceitful tongue.

Romans 16:18 - For they that are such serve not our Lord Jesus Christ/ MASTER YAHWEH MESSIAH, but their own belly; and by good words and fair speeches deceive the hearts of the simple.

INCARNATION –Yahweh took on the flesh who is Spirit to be made visible to man and to become the offered Lamb for the transgressions of man.

Psalms 36:3 - The words of his mouth are iniquity and deceit: he hath left off to be wise, and to do good.

Psalms 43:1 - Judge me, Yahweh, and plead my cause against an unrighteous nation: O deliver me from the deceitful and unjust man.

Psalms 101:7 and plead my cause, No one who practices deceit shall dwell in my house; no one who utters lies shall continue before my eyes."

All the denominations in Christianity teach their own belief on how a person obtains salvation. There is only one truth to how a person can obtain salvation when that time comes again, and that is when Yahweh fills people with His Spirit, which is what gives salvation to a person. THERE IS NO SALVATION AVAILABLE TODAY IN THIS DECEITFUL, LYING, SATANIC WORLD. You are being lied to if they tell you that there is.

Matthew 7:21-23

21 "Not everyone who says to me, MASTER, MASTER,' will enter the Kingdom of Yahweh, but the one who does the will of my Father who is in heaven.

22 On that day many will say to me, 'MASTER, MASTER, did we not prophesy in your name, and cast out demons in your name, and do many mighty works in your name?'

23 And then will I declare to them, 'I never knew you; depart from me, you workers of iniquity."

CHAPTER 27

THE KINGDOM OF YAHWEH

Matthew 4:17

¹⁷ From that time Jesus/ IMMANUEL began to preach/TEACH, and to say, repent: for the kingdom of heaven/YAHWEH is at hand.

Luke 17:20-21

20 And when he was demanded of the Pharisees, when the kingdom of Yahweh should come, **he answered them and said, the kingdom of Yahweh cometh not with observation:**

21 Neither shall they say, Lo here! or, lo there! for, behold, the kingdom of Yahweh is within you.

1 Corinthians 15:24

24 Then cometh the end, when he shall have delivered up the Kingdom to Yahweh, even the Father; when he shall have put down all rule and all authority and power.

25 For he must reign, till he hath put all enemies under his feet.

26 The last enemy that shall be destroyed is death.

27 For he hath put all things under his feet. But when he saith all things are put under him, it is manifest that he is excepted, which did put all things under him.

28 And when all things shall be subdued unto him, then shall the Son also himself be subject unto him that put all things under him, that Yahweh may be all in all.

Luke 12:32 Fear not, little flock; **your Father's good pleasure to give you the kingdom.**

Matthew 6:33 But **seek ye first the kingdom of Yahweh, and his righteousness; and all these things shall be added unto you.**

John 18:36 Immanuel answered, my kingdom is not of this world: if my kingdom were of this world, then would my servants fight, that I should not be delivered to the Jews: **but now is my kingdom not from hence.**

John 3:5 Immanuel answered, Verily, verily, I say unto thee, **except a man be born of the Spirit, he cannot enter into the kingdom of Yahweh.**

Baptism by water has saved no one; the Baptism with the infilling of Yahweh's Spirit is what gave and will give again, a person Salvation and how a person enters Yahweh's Kingdom.

Matthew 12:28 But **if I cast out devils by the Spirit of Yahweh, then the kingdom of Yahweh has come unto you. THE EVIDENCE!**

Luke 10:99 And heal the sick that are therein, and say unto them, the kingdom of Yahweh has come nigh unto you. THE EVIDENCE!

ACTS 14:22 Confirming the souls of the disciples, and exhorting them to continue in the faith, and that we must through much tribulation enter the **kingdom of God/YAHWEH.**

I want to prove something here, and it is when it comes to Yahweh and his Word, it was always called the Word and not Bible or Scriptures or any other word, IN THE WORD.

John 1:1

1 In the beginning was the Word, and the Word was with Yahweh, and the Word was Yahweh.

This is why his Word is called the Word of Yahweh, and his spoken Word can never be changed; only the written Word could be changed, and it was, by Constantine in the 4th century, it was propagandized to fit his pagan Christianity.

Bible comes from Biblos, a female deity no other than Semiramis, Nimrod's wife/mother. Jerome, in 400 C.E., used the word Bible for his Latin Vulgate, based on paganism and is the root of all the translations, which means a collection of books, and was the first to use that word. It may have found its way into a few translations since there are so many of them. Otherwise, it was used just on the cover. The word Scriptures came into use later and took the place of the Bible and means Writings. The latest term being used is the word Gospel which has different meanings within Christianity. The true meaning comes from paganism and means God Spell. **The main thing is to never call any of them the Word, they are not the true Word of Yahweh.**

CHAPTER 28

ZION IS THE HARLOT:

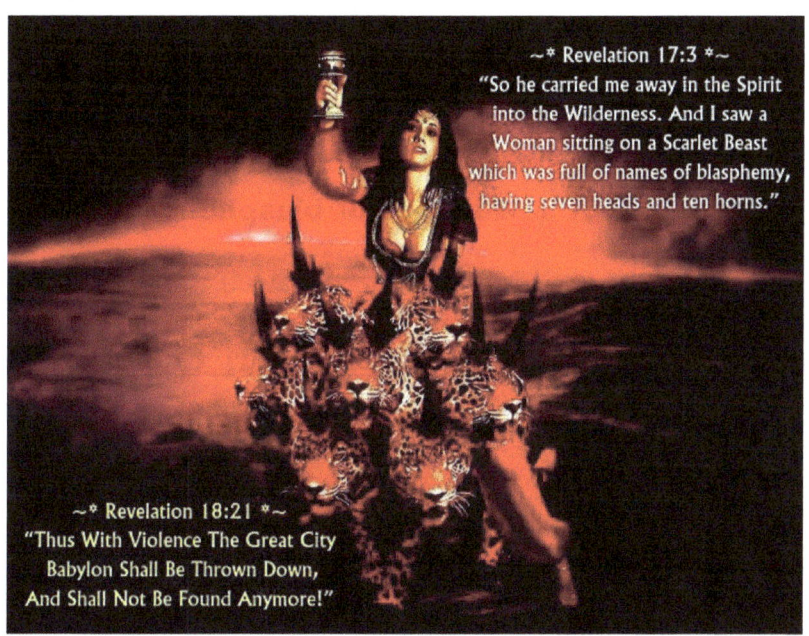

REVELATION CHAPTER 17 IS ALL ABOUT HOW ZION BECOMES THE CAPITAL CITY OF THE WORLD WHEN THE POPE MOVES HIS THRONE THERE AND THE PAPACY RULES THE WORLD FROM ZION DURING THE 3 1/2 YEAR TRIBULATION PERIOD WHEN THE PAPACY AND CHRISTIANS KILL THE ELECT OF YAHWEH MESSIAH:

THEN: 2 Thessalonians 1:7-9 And to you who are troubled rest with us, when Yahweh shall be revealed from heaven with his mighty Messengers, In flaming fire taking vengeance on them that know not Yahweh, and that obey not the Word of our Yahweh Messiah: Who shall be punished with everlasting destruction from the presence of Yahweh, and from the esteem of his power; FIRST LAKE OF FIRE

Revelation 17: 1-6

1 And there came one of the seven Messengers which had the seven vials, and talked with me, saying unto me, come hither; I will shew unto thee the judgment of the great whore that sitteth upon many waters:

2 With whom the kings of the earth have committed fornication, and the inhabitants of the earth have been made drunk with the wine of her fornication.

3 So he carried me away in the spirit into the wilderness: and **I saw a woman <u>sit upon a scarlet-colored beast</u>, full of names of blasphemy, having seven heads and ten horns.**

4 And **the woman was <u>arrayed in purple and scarlet color</u>, and decked with gold and precious stones and pearls, <u>having a golden cup in her hand full of abominations and filthiness of her fornication:</u>**

The judgment of the Great Whore that sitteth on many waters. Zion is this Great Whore,

Revelation 17:15 <u>And he saith unto me, **the waters which thou sawest, where the whore sitteth,** are peoples, and multitudes, and nations, and tongues.</u>

Zion becomes the Capital City of the world when the Pope moves his throne to Zion and sits it inside the Temple of God inside the facade of the Dome of the Rock, and the Papacy rules the world from Zion. There will be no third House of Yahweh built until the Millennial Kingdom when Yahweh Messiah builds it himself.

TYPE IN OR GOOGLE IT.

https://ivarfjeld.com/2009/07/21/the-papal-throne-to-shift-from-rome-to-jerusalem/

Revelation 17:18 "The great city that rules over the kings of the earth."

This is the Abomination of Desolation that the scriptures speak of. (THIS IS WHAT WILL MAKE ZION DESOLATE, IT BEING THE ARMAGEDDON WAR, AND ZION OF THIS EARTH WILL NEVER EXIST AGAIN AFTER THAT.) having a golden cup in her hand full of abominations and filthiness of her fornication: She lays down with the Papacy that has absorbed all the world religions into its world religion of Christianity, which makes Zion the mother of Harlots. Zion has laid down with this Babylonian religious system started by Nimrod, and he was the first Pontifex Maximus/Pope and who started all the pagan Babylonian religions when he turned his back on Yahweh, so no wonder Zion became the end time Babylon; why her destruction will be required of her, this is her end for becoming a Harlot after turning away from Yahweh. Zion becomes a wasteland, and her end.

Revelation 18:2 And he cried mightily with a strong voice, saying, <u>Babylon the great is fallen, is fallen, and is become the habitation of devils, and the hold of every foul spirit, and a cage of every unclean and hateful bird.</u>

REVELATION 19:17,21 And I saw an Messenger standing in the sun; and he cried with a loud voice, **saying to all the fowls that fly in the midst of heaven, <u>Come and gather yourselves together unto the supper of the great Yahweh;</u>**

21 And the remnant were slain with the sword of Him that sat upon the horse, whose sword proceeded out of His mouth. **<u>And all the fowls were filled with their flesh.</u>**

Zechariah 18:3 Thus saith Yahweh; I am returned unto Zion and will dwell in the midst of Zion: and Zion shall be called a city of truth; and the mountain of Yahweh of hosts the righteous mountain.

Exodus 26:36 **And thou shalt make a hanging for the door of the tent, of blue, and <u>purple, and scarlet,</u> and fine twined linen, wrought with needlework.** Is this why the Catholic church adopted these colors to help to deceive people into looking at her as the great harlot and not Zion the true Harlot

Yahweh used purple and scarlet on the cloth used for the doorway of his tabernacle. Purple was used for royalty and why they put a purple robe on Immanuel because he said he was the King of the Jews and the reason for putting a crown of thorns upon his head.

John 19:2 **And the soldiers platted a crown of thorns, and put it on his head,** and they **put on him a <u>purple robe</u>,**

5 And upon her forehead *was* a name written, MYSTERY, BABYLON THE GREAT, THE MOTHER OF HARLOTS AND ABOMINATIONS OF THE EARTH.

6 And I saw the woman drunken with the blood of the Elect, and with the blood of the martyrs of Yahweh: and when I saw her, I wondered with great admiration.

<u>**Revelation 17:4-7**</u>

Exodus 26:36 King James Version 36 **And thou shalt make a hanging** for the door of the tent, of blue, and purple, and scarlet, and fine twined linen, wrought with needlework.

Revelation 17:7-14

Verse 7. And the Messenger said unto me, wherefore didst thou marvel? I will tell thee the mystery of the woman, and of the BEAST that carrieth her, which hath the seven heads and ten horns.

Verse 8. The BEAST that thou sawest WAS, and IS NOT; and shall ascend out of the bottomless pit {The Grave}, and go into perdition {state of eternal punishment}: and *they that dwell on the earth shall wonder, whose names were not written in the book of life from the foundation of the world,* <u>when they behold the BEAST that WAS, and IS NOT and YET IS</u>.

Verse 9. And here is *the mind which hath wisdom.* **The seven heads are seven mountains, on which the woman sitteth.**

Zion is the woman that rides upon this religious Empire BEAST.

Jerusalem sits on 7 mountains.

The Seven Mountains of ZION:

1. Mount Zion

2. Mount Moriah

3. Mount Ophel

4. Mount Bezetha

5. Mount Acra

6. Mount Gareb

7. Mount Goath

All have parts that sit within the walls of Zion.

Verse 10. *And there are seven kings: five are fallen,*

1. **Egyptian EMPIRE**

2. **Assyrian EMPIRE**

3. **Babylonian EMPIRE**

4. **Medo - Persian EMPIRE**

5. **Grecian EMPIRE**

and one is,

6. **Roman EMPIRE -** At the time of John's writing of Revelation.

2 Thessalonians 2:3-12

3. Let no man deceive you by any means: for that day shall not come, except there come a falling away first, and that man of transgression be revealed, the son of perdition;

4. Who opposeth and exalteth himself above all that is called a deity, or that is worshipped; so that he as a deity sitteth in the temple of God / a deity, shewing himself that he is a deity.

5. Remember ye not, that, when I was yet with you, I told you these things?

6. And now ye know what withholdeth that he might be revealed in his time.

7. For the mystery of iniquity doth already work: only he who now letteth will let, until he be taken out of the way.

NOTE: The Roman Empire went from a secular to a religious government, and who was the head of it? The POPE. Emperor Constantine started Christianity and started this new form of government for the Roman Empire and became the first Pope over Christianity and. Pontifex Maximus is traced back to Nimrod, the first one he started paganism and was the one who turned his back on Yahweh and was the first false messiah. The emperor became the Pope.

8. And then shall that Wicked be revealed, whom Yahweh shall consume with the spirit of his mouth, and shall destroy with the brightness of his coming:

9. Even him, who's coming is after the working of Satan with all power and signs and lying wonders,

10. And with all deceivableness of unrighteousness in them that perish; because they received not the love of the truth, that they might be saved.

11. And for this cause Yahweh shall send them strong delusion, that they should believe a lie:

12. That they all might be damned who believed not the truth but had pleasure in unrighteousness.

NOTE: The great falling away took place back in the days of Peter and Paul. Mark 16:16 He that believeth and is baptized shall be saved, but he that believeth not shall be damned. [It was not water baptism that saved them but the baptism of Yahweh's Spirit.]

2 Thessalonians 2:10,13

10 And with all deceivableness of unrighteousness in them that perish; because they received not the love of the truth, that they might be saved.

13 But we are bound to give thanks always to Yahweh for you, brethren beloved of Yahweh, because Yahweh hath from the beginning chosen you to salvation through sanctification of the Spirit and belief of the truth:

The Anti-Messiah and Man of Transgressions were revealed already in the days of Peter and Paul, yet people today don't realize who it is, and they are still waiting for his appearance. The last Pope will rule from Zion.

REVELATION CHAPTER 18 – IS ALL ABOUT ZION

THIS WHOLE CHAPTER IS SPEAKING ABOUT ZION, THE CITY CALLED JERUSALEM TODAY:

1 And after these things I saw another Messenger come down from heaven, having great power; and the earth was lightened with his righteousness.

2 And he cried mightily with a strong voice, saying, Babylon the great is fallen, is fallen, and is become the habitation of devils, and the hold of every foul spirit, and a cage of every unclean and hateful bird.

3 For all nations have drunk of the wine of the wrath of her fornication, and the kings of the earth have committed fornication with her, and the merchants of the earth are waxed rich through the abundance of her delicacies.

4 And I heard another voice from heaven, saying, Come out of her, my people, that ye be not partakers of her transgressions, and that ye receive not of her plagues.

5 For her transgressions have reached unto heaven, and Yahweh hath remembered her iniquities.

6 Reward her even as she rewarded you, and double unto her double according to her works: in the cup which she hath filled fill to her double.

7 How much she hath glorified herself, and lived deliciously, so much torment and sorrow give her: for she saith in her heart, I sit a queen, and am no widow, and shall see no sorrow.

8 Therefore shall her plagues come in one day, death, and mourning, and famine; and she shall be utterly burned with fire: for strong is Yahweh who judgeth her.

9 And the kings of the earth, who have committed fornication and lived deliciously with her, shall bewail her, and lament for her, when they shall see the smoke of her burning,

10 Standing afar off for the fear of her torment, saying, alas, alas that great city Babylon, that mighty city! <u>for in one hour is thy judgment come.</u>

11 And the merchants of the earth shall weep and mourn over her; for no man buyeth their merchandise anymore:

12 The merchandise of gold, and silver, and precious stones, and of pearls, and fine linen, and purple, and silk, and scarlet, and all thyine wood, and all manner vessels of ivory, and all manner vessels of most precious wood, and of brass, and iron, and marble,

13 And cinnamon, and odors, and ointments, and frankincense, and wine, and oil, and fine flour, and wheat, and beasts, and sheep, and horses, and chariots, and slaves, and souls of men.

14 And the fruits that thy soul lusted after are departed from thee, and all things which were dainty and goodly are departed from thee, and thou shalt find them no more at all.

15 The merchants of these things, which were made rich by her, shall stand afar off for the fear of her torment, weeping and wailing,

16 And saying, alas, alas that great city, that was clothed in fine linen, and purple, and scarlet, and decked with gold, and precious stones, and pearls!

17 For in one hour so great riches come to naught. And every shipmaster, and all the company in ships, and sailors, and as many as trade by sea, stood afar off,

18 And cried when they saw the smoke of her burning, saying, What city is like unto this great city!

19 And they cast dust on their heads, and cried, weeping, and wailing, saying, alas, alas that great city, wherein were made rich all that had ships in the sea by reason of her costliness! for in one hour is she made desolate.

20 Rejoice over her, thou heaven, and ye apostles and prophets; for Yahweh hath avenged you on her.

21 And a mighty Messenger took up a stone like a great millstone, and cast it into the sea, saying, thus with violence shall that great city Babylon be thrown down, and shall be found no more at all.

22 And the voice of harpers, and musicians, and of pipers, and trumpeters, shall be heard no more at all in thee; and no craftsman, of whatsoever craft he be, shall be found any more in thee; and the sound of a millstone shall be heard no more at all in thee;

23 And the light of a candle shall shine no more at all in thee; and the voice of the bridegroom and of the bride shall be heard no more at all in thee: for thy merchants were the great men of the earth; for by thy sorceries were all nations deceived.

24 And in her was found the blood of prophets, and of elect, and of all that were slain upon the earth.

Revelation 18:10,17,19,21

10. IN ONE HOUR IS THY JUDGMENT COME.

17. IN ONE HOUR...RICHES COME TO NOUGHT.

19. IN ONE HOUR IS SHE MADE DESOLATE|

21. WITH VIOLENCE ZION IS THROWN DOWN.

ZECHARIAH 2: 7-13

7 <u>Deliver thyself</u>, **O Zion, that dwellest with the daughter of Babylon.**

8 For thus saith Yahweh of hosts; After the glory hath **he sent me unto the nations which spoiled you:** <u>for he that toucheth you toucheth the apple of his eye.</u>

⁹ For, behold, **I will shake mine hand upon them, and they shall be a spoil to their servants: and ye shall know that Yahweh of hosts hath sent me.**

¹⁰ **Sing and rejoice, O daughter of Zion: for, lo, I come, and I will dwell in the midst of thee, saith Yahweh.**

¹¹ **And many nations shall be joined to Yahweh in that day, and shall be my people: and I will dwell in the midst of thee**, and **thou shalt know that Yahweh of hosts hath sent me unto thee.**

¹² And **Yahweh shall inherit Judah his portion in the righteous land**, **and shall choose Zion again.**

¹³ **Be silent, O all flesh, before Yahweh: for he is raised up out of his righteous habitation.**

THE END OF ZION HERE ON EARTH, THAT IS CALLED JERUSALEM TODAY.

Revelation 18:22-23

22 **And the voice of harpers, and musicians, and of pipers, and trumpeters, shall be heard no more at all in thee; and no craftsman, of whatsoever craft** *he be*, **shall be found any more in thee; and the sound of a millstone shall be heard no more at all in thee;**

²³ **And the light of a candle shall shine no more at all in thee; and the voice of the bridegroom and of the bride shall be heard no more at all in thee: for thy merchants were the great men of the earth; for by thy sorceries were all nations deceived.**

Jeremiah 4:6 Set up the standard toward Zion: retire, stay not: for I will bring evil from the north, and a great destruction.

Revelation 18:2 And he cried mightily with a strong voice, saying, Babylon the great is fallen, is fallen, and is become the habitation of devils, and the hold of every foul spirit, and a cage of every unclean and hateful bird.

ZION LAYS DOWN WITH THE PAPACY AND BECOMES THE CAPITAL CITY OF THE WORLD

Papacy Agendas for a Global Government: Illegal Alien Agenda, Universal Healthcare Agenda, Catholic Take Over of Public Schools Agenda, Taking over all Healthcare and Hospitals Agenda, Earth Warming Agenda, World Justice System, Spreading the Wealth Agenda, U.N. Authority Agenda, 10 World Unions Agenda, One World Order Agenda, Social Justice or Reform Agenda, Homosexual Agenda, Muslim Agenda, Gun Control Agenda, Planned Third World War 3 Agenda, the next big event and the last years before we meet our Creator, World Government, World Religion, World Army, International Police Force, World Central Bank and Monetary System Agenda, World Court, Global Taxation, Homosexual Agenda/LGBT/ Transgender Sex Changes, World Currency, Population Control Agenda, Common Core Agenda, Downfall of the United States Agenda. No more Property Ownership Agenda. These are all the Vatican's agendas for a World Government.

The Oxford World Christian Encyclopedia, which Catholics use to claim there are thousands of Protestant denominations, also says this about Eastern Orthodox and Roman Catholic denominations. There are 781 "Orthodox" denominations (i.e., Eastern Orthodoxy), predicting 887 by the year 2025. 242 "Roman Catholic" denominations for 2000, predicting 245 by the year 2025. **YOUR LITTLE PARAGRAPH PROVES THAT CHRISTIANITY IS NOTHING BUT PAGAN NIMROD WORSHIP, ALONG WITH THE REST OF CHRISTIANITY. YAHWEH MESSIAH IS A FAITH WITH ONLY ONE TRUTH.**

CATHOLICS WILL END UP TAKING OVER THE HOSPITALS' AND SCHOOLS AGENDA

We were forewarned:

Abraham Lincoln,

"I am not happy about the rebirth of the Jesuits. Swarms of them will present themselves under more disguises ever taken by even a chief of the Bohemians, as printers, writers, publishers, schoolteachers, etc. If ever an association of people deserved eternal damnation, on this earth and in hell, it is this society of Loyola."(John Adams, 1816). Abraham Lincoln said: "If the Protestants of the North and the South could learn what the priests, nuns, and monks, who daily land on our shores, under the pretext of preaching their religion, were doing in our schools and hospitals, as emissaries of the Pope and the other despots of Europe, to undermine our institutions and alienate the hearts of our people from our Republic.

ABRAHAM LINCOLN I conceal what I know, on that subject, from the knowledge of the nation; for if the people knew the whole truth, this war would turn into a religious war, and it would, at once, take a tenfold more savage and bloody character, it would become merciless as all religious wars are. It would become a war of extermination on both sides. The Protestants of both the North and the South would surely unite to exterminate the priests and the Jesuits if they could hear what Professor Morse has said to me of the plots made in the very city of Rome to destroy this Republic and if they could learn how the priests, the nuns, and the monks, which daily land on our shores, under the pretext of preaching their religion, instructing the people in their schools, taking care of the sick in the hospitals, are nothing else but the emissaries of the Pope, of Napoleon, and the other despots of Europe, to undermine our institutions, alienate the hearts of our people from our constitution, and our laws, destroy our schools, and prepare a reign of anarchy here as they have done in Ireland, in Mexico, in Spain, and wherever there are any people who want to be free, etc." SO TRUE MORE SO TODAY!

Matthew 24:24

24: For there shall arise false Messiahs (Jesus, Lord, God, Christ, Allah, Buddah, Adonai, etc., and false prophets, (Preachers, Ministers, Evangelist, Priests, Rabbi's, etc.) and shall show great signs and wonders; insomuch that, if it were possible, they shall deceive the very elect.

Revelation 12:4,5,7,8,9

4. And his tail drew the third part of the stars of heaven, and did cast them to the earth: and the dragon stood before the woman which was ready to be delivered, for to devour her child as soon as it was born.

5. And she brought forth a man child, who was to rule all nations with a rod of iron: and her child was caught up unto Yahweh, and to His throne.

Now, in the next verse 7, watch what happens AFTER the child is caught up unto Yahweh and His Throne.

7. And there was war in heaven: Michael and his Messengers fought against the dragon; and the dragon fought and his messengers,

8. And prevailed not; NEITHER WAS THEIR PLACE FOUND ANY MORE IN HEAVEN.

9. And the great dragon WAS CAST OUT, that old serpent, called the Devil, and Satan, which DECEIVETH THE WHOLE WORLD: HE WAS CAST OUT into the earth, AND HIS MESSENGERS WERE CAST OUT WITH HIM.

See how Satan has deceived the WHOLE WORLD since the days of Peter and Paul?

John 8:24-28

24. I said therefore unto you, that ye shall die in your transgressions: for if ye believe not that I am He (YAHWEH), ye shall die in your transgressions.

28. Then said Immanuel unto them, when ye have lifted up the Son of man, then shall ye know that I am He (YAHWEH), and that I do nothing of myself; but as my Father hath taught me, I speak these things.

John 14:7,8

7. If ye had known me, ye should have known my Father also: and from henceforth ye know him, and have seen him.

8. Philip told him, "Master, show us the Father, and that will satisfy us."

9. Immanuel saith unto him, Have I been so long time with you, and yet hast thou not known me, Philip? he that hath seen me hath seen the Father; and how sayest thou then, Shew us the Father?

Philippians 2:6 Who, being in the form of Yahweh, thought it not robbery to be equal with Yahweh:

You must get out of Christianity, it will be the One World Religion, and Yahweh Messiah is calling a people out for His Name's sake.

Matthew 10:36 And a man's foes shall be they of his own household.

The Oxford World Christian Encyclopedia, which Catholics use to claim there are thousands of Protestant denominations, also says this about Eastern Orthodox and Roman Catholic denominations. There are 781 "Orthodox" denominations (i.e., Eastern Orthodoxy), predicting 887 by the year 2025. 242 "Roman Catholic" denominations for 2000, predicting 245 by the year 2025. YOUR LITTLE SENTENCE PROVES IT IS NOTHING BUT PAGAN NIMROD WORSHIP, ALONG WITH THE REST OF CHRISTIANITY.

The Council of Nicea discussed a 40-day *Lenten* season of fasting;... Until the 600s, Lent began on Quadragesima (Fortieth) Sunday, but Gregory the Great (c.540-604) moved it to a Wednesday, now called Ash Wednesday. In the fifth century, St.

Augustine declared that all unbaptized babies went to hell upon death. By the Middle Ages, the idea was softened to suggest a less severe fate, limbo. Ash Wednesday. **LENT IS A PAGAN HOLIDAY TO DO WITH NIMROD, TAMMUZ AND SEMIRAMIS.**

Rev. 19:11-13

11: And I saw heaven opened, and behold a white horse; and he that sat upon him was called Faithful and True, and in righteousness he doth judgeth and make war.

12: His eyes were as a flame of fire, and on his head were many crowns; and he had a name written, that no man knew, but he himself.

13. And he was clothed with a vesture dipped in blood: and his name is called The Word of Yahweh.

Rev. 3:12 Him that overcometh will I make a pillar in the House of Yahweh and he shall go no more out: and I will write upon him the name of Yahweh, and the name of the city of Yahweh, which is **New Zion, which cometh down out of heaven from Yahweh:** and **I will write upon him my new name.**

In the next two verses you will see Yahweh was His name during Creation.

Isaiah 64:8 But now, **O Yahweh, thou art our father, we are the clay, and thou our potter, and we all are the work of thy hand.**

Isaiah 37:16 O **Yahweh of hosts**, Almighty of Judaea, that dwellest between the cherubims, thou art the Almighty, even thou alone, of all the kingdoms of the earth: **thou hast made heaven and earth.**

Yahweh is his name when He returns.

Zech. 8 Thus saith Yahweh; I am returned unto Zion, and will dwell in the midst of Zion: and Zion shall be called a city of truth; and the mountain of Yahweh of hosts the righteous mountain.

Yahweh, His name during the Millennium.

Jer. 16:19 & 21

19: O Yahweh, my strength, and my fortress, and my refuge in the day of affliction, the Gentiles shall come unto thee from the ends of the earth, and shall say, surely our fathers have inherited lies, vanity, and things wherein there is no profit.

21: Therefore, behold, I will this once cause them to know, I will cause them to know mine hand and my might; and they shall know that my name is Yahweh.

Ezekiel 48:35

35: and the name of the city from that day shall be: Yahweh is there.

Yahweh, His name on the New Earth.

Rev. 21:1-4

1: And <u>**I saw a new heaven and a new earth: for the first heaven and the first earth were passed away; and there was no more sea.**</u>

2: And I <u>**John saw the righteous city, new Zion, coming down from Yahweh out of heaven, prepared as a bride adorned for her husband.**</u>

3: **And I heard a great voice out of heaven saying, Behold, Yahweh is with men, and he will dwell with them and be their Father.**

4: And <u>**Yahweh shall wipe away all tears from their eyes; and there shall be no more death, neither sorrow, nor crying, neither shall there be any more pain: for the former things are passed away.**</u>

<u>**THESE VERSES ABOVE PROVE THAT NEW ZION WILL COME DOWN ON THE NEW EARTH, NOT THIS EARTH.**</u>

2 Corinthians 11:15

"Therefore, it is no great thing if his ministers also been transformed as the ministers of righteousness; whose end shall be according to their works.

Matthew 24:24

24: For there shall arise false Messiahs (Jesus, Lord, God, Christ, Allah, Buddah, Adonai, etc., and false prophets, (Preachers, Ministers, Pastors,Evangelist, Priests, Rabbi's, etc.) and shall show great signs and wonders; insomuch that, **if it were possible, they shall deceive the very elect.**

Revelation 12:4,5,7,8,9

4. And his tail drew the third part of the stars of heaven, and did cast them to the earth: and the dragon stood before the woman which was ready to be delivered, for to devour her child as soon as it was born.

5. And she brought forth a man child, who was to rule all nations with a rod of iron: and her child was caught up unto Yahweh, and to His throne.

Now, in the next verse 7, watch what happens AFTER the child is caught up unto Yahweh and His Throne.

7. And there was war in heaven: Michael and his Messengers fought against the dragon; and the dragon fought and his messengers,

8. And prevailed not; NEITHER WAS THEIR PLACE FOUND ANY MORE IN HEAVEN.

9. And the great dragon WAS CAST OUT, that old serpent, called Satan, which DECEIVETH THE WHOLE WORLD: HE WAS CAST OUT into the earth, AND HIS MESSENGERS WERE CAST OUT WITH HIM.

See how Satan has deceived the WHOLE WORLD since the days of Peter and Paul?

John 8:24-28

24. I said therefore unto you, that ye shall die in your transgressions: for if ye believe not that I am He (YAHWEH), ye shall die in your transgressions.

28. Then said Immanuel unto them, When ye have lifted up the Son of man, then shall ye know that I am He (YAHWEH), and that I do nothing of myself; but as my Father hath taught me, I speak these things.

John 14:7,8

7. If ye had known me, ye should have known my Father also: and from henceforth ye know him, and have seen him.

8. Philip told him, "Master, show us the Father, and that will satisfy us."

9. Immanuel saith unto him, Have I been so long time with you, and yet hast thou not known me, Philip? he that hath seen me hath seen the Father; and how sayest thou then, Shew us the Father?

Philippians 2:6 Who, being in the form of Yahweh, thought it not robbery to be equal with Yahweh:

You must get out of Christianity; it will be the One World Religion, and Yahweh Messiah is calling a people out for His Name's sake.

Matthew 10:36 And a man's foes shall be they of his own household.

The New Name

The name Jesus is a proven lie. Christians are now trying other ways to condone this lie. You hear things like this:

1. He has many names, so it does not matter what you call him.

2. It does not matter what you call him, He knows who you mean.

3. Forget the name, it's the Spirit that's in you that matters.

The next two given are the latest I have heard.

4. He was given the name Jesus by the Greeks when Joseph and Mariam took him to Egypt, because Herod was looking for a child named Immanuel.

5. The name doesn't matter because, in Revelation, it says He will have a new name. Only He knows.

This is the one I would like to address at this time, since the others are proven false in other studies.

His name, Yahweh, never changes, so it must be an office, a new office such as; Name then Office: Yahweh – Nissi, our banner; Yahweh – Yireh, will provide; Name and Office; Yahweh – Messiah, anointed one; etc. So, whatever that office is, only he knows it.

Here is a scenario: say you painted an oil painting, and it ended up being worth 1 million dollars, and someone came along and put another name on it to give that name the credit for what you had done, AND THEY SOLD IT AND RECEIVED THE MONEY AND FAME THAT SHOULD HAVE WENT TO YOU, WOULD YOU BE UPSET?, THAT IS EXACTLY WHAT WAS DONE TO IMMANUEL'S NAME THAT THEY EXCHANGED IT FOR THE PAGAN NAME JESUS AND WHY PEOPLE BELIEVE AND USE THAT NAME STILL TODAY. THE PERSONAGE OF IMMANUEL BECAME THE PERSONAGE UNDER THE NAME JESUS, A FALSEHOOD TAUGHT AS THE TRUTH.

CHAPTER 29

VERSES WITH JUDAEA AND OTHER WORDS CORRECTED: SO, COMPARE

Matthew 3:1 In those days came John the Baptist, teaching in the wilderness of Judaea,

Matthew 3:5 Then went out to him Zion, and all Judaea, and all the region round about Jordan,

Matthew 4:25 And there followed him great multitudes of people from Galilee, and [from] Decapolis, and [from] Zion, and [from] Judaea, and [from] beyond Jordan.

Matthew 19:1 And it came to pass, [that] when Immanuel had finished these sayings, he departed from Galilee, and came into the coasts of Judaea beyond Jordan;

Matthew 24:16 Then let them which be in Judaea flee into the mountains:

Mark 1:5 And there went out unto him all the land of Judaea, and they of Zion, and were all baptized of him in the river of Jordan, confessing their transgressions.

Mark 3:7 But Immanuel withdrew himself with his disciples to the sea: and a great multitude from Galilee followed him, and from Judaea.

Mark 10:1 And he arose from thence, and cometh into the coasts of Judaea by the farther side of Jordan: and the people resort unto him again; and, as he was wont, he taught them again.

Mark 13:14 But when ye shall see the abomination of desolation, spoken of by Daniel the prophet, standing where it ought not, (let him that readeth understand,) then let them that be in Judaea flee to the mountains:

Luke 1:5 There was in the days of Herod, the king of Judaea, a certain priest named Zacharias, of the course of Abia: and his wife [was] of the daughters of Aaron, and her name [was] Elisabeth.

Luke 1:65 And fear came on all that dwelt round about them: and all these sayings were noised abroad throughout all the hill country of Judaea.

Original Verse: Luke 2:4 And Joseph also went up from Galilee, out of the city of Nazareth, into Judaea, unto the city of David, which is called Bethlehem; (because he was of the house and lineage of David:)

Corrected Verse: Luke 2:4 And Joseph also went up from the city of Nazareth, unto the city of David, which is called Bethlehem; (because he was of the house and lineage of David:)

Explanation of: Luke 2:4 was really messed with to hide the truth of him going to the Bethlehem of Galilee and not to the Bethlehem of Judah, which Christianity teaches as the birthplace, which is a lie. Compare the 2 verses, I use the King James. Bethlehem is in Galilee, not Judaea.

Luke 3:1 Now in the fifteenth year of the reign of Tiberius Caesar, Pontius Pilate being governor of Judaea, and **Herod the {son of Herod the Great}** being tetrarch of Galilee, and his brother Philip tetrarch of Ituraea and of the region of Trachonitis, and Lysanias the tetrarch of Abilene,

Luke 5:17 And it came to pass on a certain day, as he was teaching, that there were Pharisees and doctors of the law sitting by, which were come out of every town of Galilee, and Judaea, and Zion: and the power of Yahweh was [present] to heal them.

Luke 6:17 And he came down with them, and stood in the plain, and the company of his disciples, and a great multitude of people out of all Judaea and Zion, and from the seacoast of Tyre and Sidon, which came to hear him, and to be healed of their diseases;

Luke 7:17 And this rumor of him went forth throughout all Judaea, and throughout all the region round about.

Luke 21:21 Then let them which are in Judaea flee to the mountains; and let them which are in the midst of it depart out; and let not them that are in the countries enter thereinto.

John 3:22 After these things came Immanuel and his disciples into the land of Judaea; and there he tarried with them and baptized.

John 4:3 He left Judaea and departed again into Galilee. John 4:47 When he heard that Immanuel was come out of Judaea into Galilee, he went unto him, and besought him that he would come down, and heal his son: for he was at the point of death.

John 4:54 This [is] again the second miracle [that] Immanuel did, when he was come out of Judaea into Galilee.

John 7:3 His brethren therefore said unto him, depart hence, and go into Judaea, that thy disciples also may see the works that thou doest.

John 11:7 Then after that saith he to [his] disciples, let us go into Judaea again.

Acts 1:8 But ye shall receive power, after that the Spirit comes upon you: and ye shall be witnesses unto me both in Zion, and in all Judaea, and in Samaria, and unto the uttermost part of the earth.

Acts 2:9 Parthians, and Medes, and Elamites, and the dwellers in Mesopotamia, and in Judaea, and Cappadocia, in Pontus, and Asia,

Acts 2:14 But Peter, standing up with the eleven, lifted up his voice, and said unto them, Ye men of Judaea, and all [ye] that dwell at Zion, be this known unto you, and hearken to my words:

Acts 8:1 And Saul was consenting unto his death. And at that time there was a great persecution against the assembly which was at Zion; and they were all scattered abroad throughout the regions of Judaea and Samaria, except the apostles.

Acts 9:31 Then had the assembly's rest throughout all Judaea and Galilee and Samaria and were edified; and walking in the fear of Yahweh, and in the comfort of the Spirit was multiplied.

Acts 10:37 That word, [I say], ye know, which was published throughout all Judaea, and began from Galilee, after the baptism which John taught;

Acts 11:1 And the apostles and brethren that were in Judaea heard that the Gentiles had also received the Word of Yahweh.

Acts 11:29 Then the disciples, every man according to his ability, determined to send relief unto the brethren which dwelt in Judaea:

Acts 12:19 And when Herod had sought for him, and found him not, he examined the keepers and commanded that [they] should be put to death. And he went down from Judaea to Caesarea, and [there] abode.

Acts 15:1 And certain men which came down from Judaea taught the brethren, [and said], Except ye be circumcised after the manner of Moses, ye cannot be saved.

Acts 21:10 And as we tarried [there] many days, there came down from Judaea a certain prophet, named Agabus.

Acts 26:20 But showed first unto them of Damascus, and at Zion, and throughout all the coasts of Judaea, and [then] to the Gentiles, that they should repent and turn to Yahweh, and do works meet for repentance.

Acts 28:21 And they said unto him, We neither received letters out of Judaea concerning thee, neither any of the brethren that came showed or spake any harm of thee.

Romans 15:31 That I may be delivered from them that do not believe in Judaea; and that my service which [I have] for Zion may be accepted of the Elect;

2 Corinthians *1:16* And to pass by you into Macedonia, and to come again out of Macedonia unto you, and of you to be brought on my way toward Judaea.

Galatians 1:22 And was unknown by face unto the assemblies of Yahweh of Judaea which were in Messiah Yahweh:

1 Thessalonians *2:14* For ye, brethren, became followers of the assemblies of Yahweh which in Judaea are in Messiah Yahweh: for ye also have suffered like things of your own countrymen, even as they [have] of the Jews:

CHAPTER 30

#2 NEW ZION

What was said about New Zion?

Who built New Zion?

Hebrews 11:10 <u>for he looked for a city which hath foundations, whose builder and maker is Yahweh.</u>

2 <u>And I John saw the righteous city, new Zion, coming down from Yahweh out of heaven, prepared as a bride adorned for her husband.</u>

10 <u>And he carried me away in the spirit to a great and high mountain, and shewed me that great city, the righteous Zion, descending out of heaven from Yahweh,</u>

Revelation 22:1-21

<u>1 And he shewed me a pure river of water of life, clear as crystal, proceeding out of the throne of Yahweh and of the Lamb.</u>

2 <u>In the midst of the street of it, and on either side of the river, was there the tree of life, which bare twelve manners of fruits, and yielded her fruit every month: and the leaves of the tree were for the healing of the nations.</u>

3 <u>And there shall be no more curse: but the throne of Yahweh and of the Lamb shall be in it; and his servants shall serve him:</u>

4 <u>And they shall see his face; and his name shall be in their foreheads.</u>

5 And there shall be no night there; and they need no candle, neither light of the sun; for Yahweh giveth them light: and they shall reign for ever and ever.

6 And he said unto me, These sayings are faithful and true: and Yahweh of the righteous prophets sent his Messenger to shew unto his servants the things which must shortly be done.

8 **And I John saw these things, and heard them. And when I had heard and seen, I fell down to worship before the feet of the Messenger which shewed me these things.**

11 He that is unjust, let him be unjust still: and he which is filthy, let him be filthy still: and he that is righteous, let him be righteous still.

13 I am Alpha and Omega, the beginning and the end, the first and the last.

14 Blessed are they that do his commandments, that they may have right to the tree of life, and may enter in through the gates into the city.

15 For without are dogs, and sorcerers, and whoremongers, and murderers, and idolaters, and whosoever loveth and maketh a lie.

16 I Yahweh have sent mine Messenger to testify unto you these things in the assemblies. I am the root and the offspring of David, and the bright and morning star.

17 And the Spirit and the bride say, Come. And let him that heareth say, Come. And let him that is athirst come. And whosoever will, let him take the water of life freely.

18 For I testify unto every man that heareth the words of the prophecy of this book, If any man shall add unto these things, God shall add unto him the plagues that are written in this book:

19 And if any man shall take away from the words of the book of this prophecy, Yahweh shall take away his part out of the book of life, and out of the righteous city, and from the things which are written in this book.

20 He which testifieth these things saith, Surely, I come quickly. Even so, come, Master Yahweh.

21 The Spirit of our Master Yahweh Messiah be with you all.

CHAPTER 31

HEALINGS ARE COMING

THESSALONIANS 5:21 Test everything hold to what is good.

HEALINGS ARE COMING

The ears that cannot hear,
The eyes that cannot see,
The mind that cannot comprehend,
Must be healed.

Your ears must hear the Word,
Your eyes must see the miracles,
Your mind must comprehend it all.
To have the faith that brings salvation,
His Spirit infilling.

When it is made available one more time,
To the living before his return,
And for those that have died,
After Constantine's rule,
That never heard his truth.

The Millennial Kingdom is for you,
To be schooled and taught by him,
The whole truth that you never had heard,

Will be given a choice to serve Satan or him,
Then Judgement brings all to an end.

By Gary W. Stanfield

Isaiah 29:18 states that on that day, **the deaf will hear the words of the book, and the eyes of the blind will see out of obscurity and darkness. The meek will increase their joy in Yahweh,** and **the poor among men will rejoice in the righteous One of Judaea.**

Isaiah 35:5 Then **the eyes of the blind shall be opened,** and **the ears of the deaf shall be unstopped.**

Isaiah 42:18 **Hear, you deaf! And look, you blind, that you may see.**

Isaiah 29:18 **And in that day shall the deaf hear the words of the book,** and **the eyes of the blind shall see out of obscurity, and out of darkness.**

Matthew 11:5 **The blind receive their sight, and the lame walk,** the **lepers are cleansed,** and **the deaf hear,** the **dead are raised up,** and the **poor have the word taught to them.**

Matthew 4:24 - And his fame went throughout all Syria: and **they brought unto him all sick people that were taken with divers diseases and torments,** and **those which were possessed with Satan, and those which were lunatick, and those that had the palsy; and he healed them.**.

Romans 12:2 - And **be not conformed to this world: but be ye transformed by the renewing of your mind, that ye may prove what is that good, and acceptable, and perfect, will of Yahweh.**

CHAPTER 32

MARIAM'S LINEAGE:

Joseph's lineage is in book 2, Paradox of "Christianity"; I am putting Mariam's genealogy in this book because you hear all these so-called scholars teaching against both of their lineages, and I'm going to prove both lineages are true for them both. Mariam's starts with Adam and Eve. Mariam, like Joseph, was also born in Bethlehem of Galilee, and she was raised in Nazareth after her family moved from Bethlehem to Nazareth. It is unclear how Joseph ended up in Nazareth, whether, like Mary, he moved there with his family at a younger age or when he was older, but must be where he and Mary had met or even at one of the Feasts that they would go back to in Bethlehem to celebrate them. Joseph and Mariam lived in Nazareth when they went to Bethlehem, 6 miles Northwest of Nazareth, where she had Immanuel; they did not go over a hundred miles with her riding on a donkey like Christianity teaches, which is proven to be just another Christian lie. Mariam's genealogy is shown in Luke Chapter 3 starting with King David up to Mariam's Father.

Mariam's genealogy ends with Joseph; I will prove why at the end of it; hers goes back to Adam and Eve. I will start with King David:

1. **King David**
2. **Nathan**
3. **Mattatha**
4. **Menan.**
5. **Melea**
6. **Eliakim**
7. **Jonan**

8. **Joseph**
9. **Judasimeon**
10. **Levi**
11. **Matthat**
12. **Jorim**
13. **Elizar**
14. **Jose**
15. **Er**
16. **Elmodam**
17. **Cosam**
18. **Addi**
19. **Melchi**
20. **Neri**
21. **Salathiel**
22. **Zorobabel**
23. **Rhesa**
24. **Joanna**
25. **Juda**
26. **Joseph**
27. **Semei**
28. **Mattathias**
29. **Maath**
30. **Nagge**
31. **Esli**
32. **Naum**
33. **Amos**
34. **Mattathias**
35. **Joseph**
36. **Janna**
37. **Melchi**
38. **Levi**

39. **Matthat**

40. **Heli / Heliachim – Mariam's Father**

41. **Joseph – Son-In-Law, Husband Of Mariam – Parents Of Immanuel #42.**

42. **Immanuel**

THIS IS THE REASON WHY JOSEPH'S NAME WAS USED AND NOT MARIAM'S:

CLARKE'S COMMENTARY ON THE BIBLE, IN PART:

"As the Hebrews never permitted women to enter into their genealogical tables, whenever a family happened to end with a daughter, instead of naming her in the genealogy, they inserted her husband, as the son of him who was but his father-in-law,"

John 6:42 They said, "Is this not Immanuel, the son of Joseph, whose father and mother we know? How can he say, "I came down from heaven?"

John 1:45 Philip found Nathanael, and said unto him, we have found him, of whom Moses in the law, and the prophets, did write, Immanuel of Nazareth, the son of Joseph.

CHAPTER 33

TIMELINE OF IMMANUEL

John the Baptist was born in 01 B.C.E.; Immanuel was born in 0 C.E. how did I come up with those years? King Herod died in 04 C.E. so Immanuel was 4 years old when Herod died. The Wisemen showed up at Joseph's and Mariam's home in Bethlehem when Immanuel was 2 years old, not at his birth. This is when Herod killed all the male babies 2 years old and younger to be sure he would have killed Immanuel; these murders took place in 2 C.E.; Joseph and Mariam were told in a dream to go to Egypt because he was looking to kill their child, this happened after the Wisemen showed up. So, they went to Egypt in 2 C.E. and was there for 2 years; Herod died in 4 C.E. this is when they were told to go to Judaea, then another dream, he was told to go to Galilee because Herod's son was ruling, Archelaus rule of Judea ended up being dismissed in 6 C.E., back in Nazareth where they lived before going to Bethlehem of Galilee about 6 miles from Nazareth and where Immanuel was born and they still lived there 2 years after Immanuel's birth. Immanuel grew up in Nazareth, fulfilling another prophecy, he shall be called a Nazarene. 30 C.E., Immanuel started his ministry in Galilee, and it spread from there; he knew that area well, and people knew him.

0 C.E.

1.) John the Baptist was born on Rosh *Hashanah,* a Jewish New Year, by their Civil Calendar.

2.) Immanuel was born. Nissan 1, the first day of Spring, and New Year's Day on the moon calendar to keep track of the new moons for each new month.

2 C.E.

1.) Wisemen showed up at his house when he was 2 years old, a toddler.

2.) The year the male babies 2 years and younger were murdered.

3.) When Joseph and Mariam went to Egypt.

4 C.E.

1.) When Herod died

2.) Joseph and Mariam went back and ended up back in Nazareth. They were in Egypt for 2 years.

Matthew 2:22-23

22 But when he heard that Archelaus did reign in Judaea in the room of his father Herod, he was afraid to go thither: notwithstanding, being warned of Yahweh in a dream, **he turned aside into the parts of Galilee:**

23 And **he came and dwelt in a city called Nazareth**: that it might be fulfilled which was spoken by the prophets, **He shall be called a Nazarene.**

3.) Herod's son ruled from 4 C.E. to 6 C.E. when he was dismissed.

12 C.E.

1.) Immanuel in Bethlehem of Galilee taught in the city courtyard.

30 C.E.

1.) Immanuel started his ministry.

33 C.E.

1.) Immanuel was killed, beaten within an inch of his life, and then hung to an Olive Tree with rope on his wrists until he died, by Jewish Law, not Roman Law.

A. COMPARING THE CHRISTIAN JESUS TO THE TRUTH OF IMMANUEL:

JESUS	IMMANUEL
Son of God, a pagan deity	Son of Yahweh
Carried the Cross	Carried a Yoke
Died by Roman Law	Died by Jewish Law
Died on a Cross	Died on an Olive Tree
Crucified, 3 nails were used.	Hung with rope tied to wrists
3 separate Crosses were used	All 3 suspended on the same Olive Tree
Died on Good Friday	Died on the Wednesday Passover
Rose on Sunday	Rose at the end of the 7th day Sabbath
36 hours in the grave	72 hours in the grave
2 nights / 1 day in the grave	3 nights / 3 days in the grave
Inherited his own name	Inherited the Father's name
Became Jesus Christ.	Became Yahweh Messiah
Christ, a sun deity	Messiah, the true word
Died for Sins	Died for Transgressions
Is an Anti- Messiah's name	Yahweh, the true Messiah's name
Is a Latinized Greek name	Immanuel is a Hebrew name.
Jesus Christ is 2 sun deities.	The name Immanuel is not pagan.
Your end, the Lake of Fire	Your end, Eternal Life

Born on December 25	**Born on Nissan 1.**
Born in Bethlehem of Judah	**Born in Bethlehem of Galilee**
Jesus riding a White Horse	**Yahweh, returning in spacecraft**
Jesus with his Saints	**Yahweh with his Messengers`**
Saints meet him in the air.	**Elect are caught up in spacecraft.**

Acts 18:28 For <u>**he mightily convinced the Jews**</u>, and that publicly, <u>**shewing by the scriptures that Immanuel was Yahweh.**</u>

CHAPTER 34

SION MEANS THE SUN; ZION IS THE CITY

JUST ANOTHER WAY TO DECEIVE PEOPLE.

(KJV) KING JAMES VERSION

(ASV) American Standard Version

(DARBY) Darby Version

(YLT) Young's Literal Translation

(HCSB) HOLMAN CHRISTIAN STANDARD BIBLE

(WEB) WEB

(BBE) Bible in Basic English

(EMB) Evangelical Mennonite Brethren

(NHEB) New Heart English Bible

Just see how many translations there are and versions; when all is said and done, one will not agree with any other one.

From Aroer, which is by the bank of the river Arnon, even unto Mount SION, which is Hermon,

KJV, ASV, DARBY, YLT, HCSB, WEB, BBE, EMB, WBS, NASB, KJ2000, JULIASMITH, ACV, NHEB

Psa 65:1

{To the chief Musician, A Psalm and Song of David.} Praise waiteth for thee, O God, in SION: and unto thee shall the vow be performed.

KJV

Matt 21:4

Now all this was done, that it might be fulfilled which was spoken by the prophet saying, Tell ye the daughter of SION,

WORSLEY

Matt 21:5

Tell ye the daughter of SION, Behold, thy King cometh unto thee, meek, and sitting upon an ass, and a colt the foal of an ass.

KJV, WBS, MOFFATT, MACE, WESLEY, HAWEIS

John 12:15

Fear not, daughter of Sion: behold, thy King cometh, sitting on an ass's colt.

KJV, YLT, WBS, MOFFATT, MACE, WESLEY, WORSLEY, HAWEIS, JULIASMITH

Rom 9:32

And why? Simply because Israel has relied not on faith but on what they could do. They have stumbled over the stone that makes men stumble ??33 as it is written, Here I lay a stone in Sion that will make men stumble, even a rock to trip them up; but he who believes in Him will never be disappointed.

MOFFATT

Rom 9:33

As it is written, Behold, I lay in Sion a stumbling stone and rock of offence: and whosoever believeth on him shall not be ashamed.

KJV, YLT, WBS, MACE, WESLEY, WORSLEY

Rom 11:26

And so all Israel shall be saved: as it is written, There shall come out of Sion the Deliverer, and shall turn away ungodliness from Jacob:

KJV, YLT, WBS, MOFFATT, MACE, WESLEY, WORSLEY, HAWEIS, JULIASMITH

Hebrews 12:22

But ye are come unto Mount Sion, and unto the city of the living God, the heavenly Jerusalem, and to an innumerable company of angels,

KJV, WBS, MOFFATT, MACE, WESLEY, WORSLEY, HAWEIS, JULIASMITH

1 Pet 2:6

Wherefore also it is contained in the scripture, Behold, I lay in Sion a chief corner stone, elect, precious: and he that believeth on him shall not be confounded.

KJV, WBS, MOFFATT, MACE, WESLEY, WORSLEY, HAWEIS

Rev 14:1

And I looked, and, lo, a Lamb stood on the mount Sion, and with him an hundred forty and four thousand, having his Father's name written in their foreheads.

KJV, YLT, WBS, MOFFATT, MACE, WESLEY, WORSLEY, JULIASMITH

"The trinity got its start in Ancient Babylon with Nimrod - Tammuz - and Semiramis being the first one. Semiramis demanded worship for both her husband and her son as well as herself. She claimed that her son was both the father and the son. Yes, he was "god the father" and "god the son" - The first divine incomprehensible trinity." – The Two Babylons; Alexander Hislop, p.51Alexander Hislop, p.51

I want to prove something here, and it being when it comes to Yahweh and his Word, it was always called the Word and not Bible or Scriptures or any other word, IN THE WORD.

John 1:1

1 In the beginning was the Word, and the Word was with Yahweh, and the Word was Yahweh.

This is why his Word is called the Word of Yahweh, and his spoken Word can never be changed; only the written Word could be changed, and it was, by Constantine in the 4th century, it was propagandized to fit his pagan Christianity.

Bible comes from Biblos, a female deity no other than Semiramis, Nimrod's wife/mother. Jerome was the first to use the word Bible in 400 C.E. He used the word Bible for his Latin Vulgate, based on paganism and is the root of all the translations, which means a collection of books, and was the first to use that word. It may have found its way into a few translations since there are so many of them. Otherwise, it was used just on the cover. The word Scriptures came into use later and took the place of using Bible and means Writings. The latest term being used is the word Gospel which has different meanings within Christianity. The true meaning comes from paganism and means "**God Spell.**" **<u>The main thing is to never call any of them the Word, they are not the true Word of Yahweh.</u>**

CHAPTER 35

THE NEW HEAVEN AND EARTH

How is the New Earth described?

2 Peter 3:13 Nevertheless we, according to his promise, look for new heavens and a new earth, wherein dwelleth righteousness.

Isaiah 64:4 For since the beginning of the world men have not heard, nor perceived by the ear, neither hath the eye seen, O Yahweh, beside thee, what he hath prepared for him that waiteth for him.

1 Corinthians 2:9 But as it is written, Eye hath not seen, nor ear heard, neither have entered into the heart of man, the things which Yahweh hath prepared for them that love him.

Isaiah 66:22 For as the new heavens and the new earth, which I will make, shall remain before me, saith Yahweh, so shall your seed and your name remain.

Isaiah 65:17 For, behold, I create new heavens and a new earth: and the former shall not be remembered, nor come into mind.

Revelation 21:1 And I saw a new heaven and a new earth: for the first heaven and the first earth were passed away; and there was no more sea.

What happened to the old heaven and earth?

Psalms 46:6 The heathen raged, the kingdoms were moved: he uttered his voice, the earth melted.

Psalms 102:25 <u>Of old hast thou laid the foundation of the earth: and the heavens are the work of thy hands.</u>

Revelation 21:4-5

4 And <u>Yahweh shall wipe away all tears from their eyes; and there shall be no more death, neither sorrow, nor crying, neither shall there be any more pain: for the former things are passed away.</u>

5 And <u>he that sat upon the throne said, Behold, I make all things new. And he said unto me, write: for these words are true and faithful.</u>

What happened to the Old Heaven and Old Earth?

2 Peter 3: 10-12

10 But <u>the day of Yahweh will come as a thief in the night; in the which the heavens shall pass away with a great noise, and the elements shall melt with fervent heat, the earth also and the works that are therein shall be burned up.</u>

11 <u>Seeing then that all these things shall be dissolved, what manner of persons ought ye to be in all righteous conversation and righteousness.</u>

12 <u>Looking for and hasting unto the coming of the day of Yahweh, wherein the heavens being on fire shall be dissolved, and the elements shall melt with fervent heat?</u>

Matthew 24:35 <u>Heaven and earth shall pass away, but my words shall not pass away.</u>

Revelation 20:11 And <u>I saw a great white throne, and him that sat on it, from whose face the earth and the heaven fled away; and there was found no place for them.</u>

Who will inherit the New Earth?

Psalms 37:9,11,22,28-,29, 34

9 For evildoers shall be cut off: but those that wait upon Yahweh, they shall inherit the earth.

11 But the meek shall inherit the earth; and shall delight themselves in the abundance of peace.

22 For such as be blessed of him shall inherit the earth; and they that be cursed of him shall be cut off.

28 For Yahweh loveth judgment, and forsaketh not his Elect; they are preserved for ever: but the seed of the wicked shall be cut off off.

29 The righteous shall inherit the land, and dwell therein for ever.

34 Wait on Yahweh, and keep his way, and he shall exalt thee to inherit the land: when the wicked are cut off, thou shalt see it.

CHAPTER 36

SATAN REPLACED WITH DEVIL, DEVILS; DEMON, DEMONS; UNCLEAN SPIRITS, EVIL SPIRITS

DEVIL/DEVILS

Q. Where did the word Devil come from?

Answer: The word "devil" comes from the Old English "deofol," which refers to a subordinate evil spirit afflicting humans. In Christian theology, it also represents the powerful spirit of evil known as Satan. The term "Satan" itself derives from the Hebrew "ha-Satan," meaning "opposer" or "adversary." The concept of Satan evolved over time and in phases. The modern English word "satan" comes from the Hebrew "sâtan," a generic noun meaning "accuser" or "adversary."

The word "Devil" in the scriptures comes from the Hebrew word "Satan," which means "adversary" or "accuser". It is used to refer to ordinary human adversaries or the heavenly accusers, noticing they have Satan and the Devil having the same meaning.

Devil was not originally present in the scriptures.

The word "devil" is not found in the Old Covenant.

SATAN WAS ORIGINALLY A MESSENGER OF YAHWEH. HE BECAME GREEDY FOR POWER, SO HE WAS NOT AN EVIL BEING UNTIL AFTER HIS FALL.

THEY ARE USING THE SAME SPELLING FOR DEVIL AS FOR THE NAME OF SATAN, WHICH PROVES IT IS USED FOR DECEIT AND IS NOT ORIGINAL TO THE WORD OF

SHAITAN IS SATAN. NOW COMPARE IT TO THE DEVIL IN THE PICTURE AT THE TOP OF THE BOTTOM ONE. THEY ARE THE SAME SPELLING.

Satan was replaced by the Devil in a lot of verses; then, the devil was changed to devils for plural; devils became demons. The reason why most Christians believe in Demon possession, especially the Pentecostals.

The word "devil" comes from the Old English "deofol," which referred to a

The Douay Rheims Bible (Catholic, same era as KJV) is based on the Latin Vulgate, and "daemonia" is listed throughout the Vulgate New Testament, yet Douay Rheims Bible also uses the wording "devils." It seems that "demon" was not a sufficiently evil enough word to use, and it was changed to "devil," which implies total evil (even though the Greek and Latin originals specifically "daemonia." It sounds like Shakespeare was using "demon" in much the way the Greeks did to imply a guiding spirit (good or evil).

Greek and Latin originals? There is no such thing; **Constantine put the written word of Yahweh from the original Hebrew and put it into Greek**, then **Jerome put those into Latin, and where they came up with that Greek and Latin lie, then Erasmus put Jerome's Latin back into Greek, and what they are calling original Greek. The Word of Yahweh was to and for the Hebrew people, not the Gentiles, until Cornelius, the first Gentile, and his family to receive salvation**

Revelation 12:9. And the great dragon was cast out, that old serpent, called SATAN which deceiveth the whole world: **he was cast out into the earth, and his messengers were cast out with him.**

1 Peter 5:8 - Be sober, be vigilant; **because your adversary *Satan*, as a roaring lion, walketh about, seeking whom he may devour:**

James 4:7 - Submit yourselves therefore to Yahweh. Resist **Satan**, and he will flee from you.

Matthew 12:22 - **Then was brought unto him one possessed with Satan, blind, and dumb: and he healed him, insomuch that the blind and dumb both spake and saw.**

Luke 8:2 - And certain women, which had been healed of evil spirits and infirmities, Mary called Magdalene, out of whom went Satan,

Ephesians 6:11-12 - **Put on the whole armor of Yahweh, that ye may be able to stand against the wiles of Satan.**

Mark 1:32 And at even, when the sun did set, **they brought unto him all that were diseased, and them that were possessed with Satan.**

James 2:19 - Thou believest that there is one Mighty One; thou doest well: **Satan** also believes, and trembles.

Luke 10:17 And the seventy returned with joy, saying, **Master, even Satan is subject unto us through thy name.**

SATAN:

Q. What is Satan in Hebrew?

Answer: **Hebrew word "Satan:**

הסטן **(hasatan)**

The Hebrew word for Satan is הסטן *(hasatan)*. It means "the adversary" and is derived from a verb meaning "to obstruct, oppose." **Another interpretation is that it means** "one who turns people astray.

Matthew 12:22: Immanuel healed a blind and dumb man **possessed by a devil**.

Matthew 12:22: Immanuel healed a blind and dumb man **possessed by Satan**.

Matthew 17:18: Immanuel rebuked **a devil** in a child, and the child was cured.

Matthew 17:18: Immanuel rebuked **Satan** in a child, and the child was cured.

Luke 8:36: A dumb man possessed by **a devil** was brought to Immanuel.

Luke 8:36: A dumb man possessed by **Satan** was brought to Immanuel.

Revelation 12:9 "And the great dragon was cast out, **called the *Devil*, and *Satan*,**

Revelation 12:9 "And the great dragon was cast out**, called *Satan*,**

2 Corinthians 12:7 And lest I should be exalted above measure through the abundance of the revelations, there was given to me a thorn in the flesh, **the messenger of Satan**

2 Corinthians 12:7And lest I should be exalted above measure through the abundance of the revelations, there was given to me a thorn in the flesh, **the messenger Satan buffet me, lest I should be exalted above measure.**

Revelation 20:2 And he laid hold on the dragon, that old serpent, which is ***Satan***, and bound him a thousand years,

Revelation 20:7 And when the thousand years are expired, ***Satan*** **shall be** loosed out of his prison,

Luke 10:18 "I beheld ***Satan*** as lightning fall from heaven."

Luke 22:3 Then entered ***Satan*** into Judas surnamed Iscariot, being of the number of the twelve.

Comment: Notice it was Satan who entered Judas. Yahweh gave Satan his power, but nowhere in scripture can I find where Yahweh gave the messengers that were kicked out of heaven with him any power to do anything, such as being a demon or anything else.

1 John 3:8 He that committeth transgression is of ***Satan***; for ***Satan*** transgresses from the beginning. For this purpose, the Son of Yahweh was manifested, that he might destroy the works of ***Satan***.

DEMON/DEMONS

Q. Where does Demon come from?

Answer: Assyria, Nimrod was an Assyrian who started paganism.

The term "demons" does not originate from Hebrew scriptures. It is a loanword from Assyria, borrowed from the Assyrian word "šēdu." In modern English versions of scriptures, "demon" is used as a transliteration of the Greek term "daimon."

ONCE AGAIN, CONSTANTINE WAS THE ONE THAT PUT THE WRITTEN WORD OF YAHWEH INTO GREEK AND PROPAGANDIZED IT TO DECEIVE THE WORLD WITH.

So it starts with the truth of Satan, then it goes from devil to devils, from there to demon and demons, then that goes to unclean spirits to evil Spirits. After Constantine, the Papacy kept the lies being added to the Christian scriptures. As you should be able to see that, the process of changing the Christian scriptures is a slow, deliberate process.

1 Corinthians 10:21 You cannot drink the cup of Yahweh and the cup of Satan; you cannot partake of the table of Yahweh and the table of Satan.

UNCLEAN SPIRITS/EVIL SPIRITS

Noah Webster translated the Bible using "demons" rather than "devils" (for evil spirits in the New Testament). They all took the place of Satan.

Luke 8:2 - And certain women, which had been healed of **evil spirits/Satan** and infirmities, Mary called Magdalene, out of whom went **Satan**,

Matthew 10:1 - And when he had called unto him his twelve disciples, he gave them power against **Satan**, to cast hIm out, and to heal all manner of sickness and all manner of disease.

The word "Devil" in the scriptures comes from the Hebrew word "Satan," which means "adversary" or "accuser". It is used to refer to ordinary human adversaries or the heavenly accuser.

Although Satan was not originally an evil being, he is now associated with lies and deceit.

The word "devil" is not found in the Old Covenant.

SATAN WAS ORIGINALLY A MESSENGER OF YAHWEH. HE BECAME GREEDY FOR POWER, SO HE WAS NOT AN EVIL BEING UNTIL AFTER HIS FALL.

The reason why Christians believe in Demon possession. I will prove it by the following verses that demons or demons are in, along with the corrected verses and those that prove that Satan is the original word.

THIS IS WHY THEY COME OUT WITH SO MANY NEW TRANSLATIONS THROUGH THE YEARS TO EXCHANGE ONE WORD FOR ANOTHER LYING WORD UNTIL ONE DAY, NO SCRIPTURES WILL BE IN AGREEMENT.

Matthew 17:18: Immanuel rebuked **a devil** in a child, and the child was cured.

Matthew 17:18: Immanuel rebuked **Satan** in a child, and the child was cured.

Luke 8:36: A dumb man possessed by **a devil** was brought to Immanuel.

Luke 8:36: A dumb man possessed by **Satan** was brought to Immanuel.

Ordinate "And the great dragon was cast out**, called the *Devil*, and *Satan*,**

Revelation 12:9 "And the great dragon was cast out**, called *Satan*,2**

Corinthians 12:7 And lest I should be exalted above measure through the abundance of the revelations, there was given to me a thorn in the flesh, **the messenger of Satan to buffet me**, lest I should be exalted above measure.

Revelation 20:2 And he laid hold on the dragon, that old serpent, which is **_Satan_**, and bound him a thousand years,

Revelation 20:7 And when the thousand years are expired, **_Satan_ shall be** loosed out of his prison,

Luke 10:18 "I beheld **_Satan_** as lightning fall from heaven."

Luke 22:3 Then entered **_Satan_** into Judas surnamed Iscariot, being of the number of the twelve.

1 John 3:8 He that committeth transgression is of **_Satan_**; for **_Satan_** transgresses from the beginning. For this purpose, the Son of Yahweh was manifested, that he might destroy the works of **_Satan_**.

Noah Webster translated the Bible using "demons" rather than "devils" (for evil spirits in the New Testament). They all took the place of Satan.

Mark 3:11 And **_Satan_**, when they/**he** saw him, fell down before him, and cried, saying, Thou art the Son of Yahweh.

Luke 8:2 - And certain women, which had been healed of **_evil spirits/Satan_** and infirmities, Mary called Magdalene, out of whom went **seven devils/ Satan**,

Matthew 10:1 - And when he had called unto him his twelve disciples, he gave them power against **_unclean spirits/Satan_**, to cast them out, and to heal all manner of sickness and all manner of disease.

2 Corinthians 12:7 or because of these surpassingly great revelations. Therefore, in order to keep me from becoming conceited, I was given a thorn in my flesh, a messenger of Satan, to torment me.

Luke 2: 3-4

³ Then entered Satan into Judas surnamed Iscariot, being of the number of the twelve.

⁴ And **he went his way, and communed with the chief priests and captains**, how he might betray him unto them.

This distinction between "demons" and "devils" is crucial in understanding the translation choices made by early Bible translators. The term "devil" conveys a complete sense of malevolence, aligning more closely with the depiction of Satan as the ultimate adversary of Yahweh. Meanwhile, "demon" in some historical contexts, such as in Greek literature, could refer to a spirit that was not necessarily evil, leading to potential ambiguity. In the New Testament, the role of these spirits, whether referred to as "devils" or "demons," underscores the ongoing battle between good and evil, as well as the pervasive influence of Satan in corrupting humanity.

Paul did not call them demons or evil spirits

Luke 22:3-4 - Satan enters Judas

Then entered Satan into Judas surnamed Iscariot, being of the number of the twelve.

⁴ And he went his way, and communed with the chief priests and captains, how he might betray him unto them.

John 13:27 And after the sop Satan entered into him. Then said Immanuel unto him, That thou doest, do quickly.

Did Judas act like he was demon-possessed, acting crazy? No!

CHAPTER 37

THE END TIME - TIMELINE:

WW3 >>>> 7 Year Peace Plan >>>> Moses and Eliyah show up in Zion to teach the whole truth to all the countries in this world - Truth is taught to every person on earth - Yahweh's Spirit poured out >>>>> Moses and Eliyah killed midway of Peace Plan >>>> Start of Tribulation Period >>>> Pope takes his power >>>>NO 3rd House of Yahweh, Dome of the Rock will be used >>>> Christianity made World Religion - Mark of the Beast given (CROSS) - Yahweh's elect persecuted and killed >>>> Armageddon >> Satan will make himself known and will help the world armies fight Yahweh and his Messengers before Yahweh's return>> Return of Yahweh >>>>Yahweh burns up all those who took the Mark of the Beast, the first Lake of Fire>>>> Millennial Kingdom on earth >>>> Satan raised from grave to deceive the world one last time >>>> White Throne Judgement >>>> 2nd Gog Magog War End of this world, it burns up with all the wicked with it,>>>> the second Lake of Fire >>>> New Heaven and Earth >>>> Yahweh lives on the New Earth with His Elect, no one goes to heaven..

I wanted to put this study in all my books in case people only read just one of them and not any of the other ones so that they would have the end-time timeline according to my studies, showing what I had come up with to help see what is coming after WW3 that will actually kick off the very last years that brings about Yahweh Messiah's return. The most important of them to me to know is when salvation is made available again for the salvation of those still alive at that time, with the latter rain of the pouring out of Yahweh's Spirit infilling that is the gift a person receives from Yahweh that gives salvation to a person that gives life everlasting.

SALVATION COMES AGAIN DURING THE 7-YEAR PEACE PLAN AFTER WW3:

THE LAST DAY TRUTH WILL BE TAUGHT TO ALL THE WORLD INHABITANTS AGAIN, IN YAHWEH'S NAME, AND THE LATTER RAIN OF YAHWEH'S SPIRIT POURED OUT AT THIS TIME, DURING THE 7 YEAR PEACE PLAN:

Revelation 14:6-7

6. And I saw another Messenger fly, in the midst of heaven, having the "Everlasting Word...to Teach unto them that dwell on the earth, and to every nation,

7. Saying with a loud voice, Fear Yahweh, and give praise to Him; for the hour of His judgment is come: and worship him that made heaven, and earth, and the sea, and the fountains of waters.

Revelation 11:3 And I will give *power* unto my two witnesses, and they shall prophesy a thousand two hundred *and* threescore days, clothed in sackcloth.

NOTE: 3 1/2 years the first 3 1/2 years of the 7-Year Peace Plan. The last 3 1/2 years is the Tribulation Period.

Malachi 4:5-6

⁵ Behold, I will send you Elijah the prophet before the coming of the great and dreadful day of Yahweh:

⁶ And he shall turn the heart of the fathers to the children, and the heart of the children to their fathers, lest I come and smite the earth with a curse.

Luke 1:17 And he shall go before him in the spirit and power of Eliyah, to turn the hearts of the fathers to the children, and the disobedient to the wisdom of the just; to make ready a people prepared for Yahweh.

Matthew 24:14 And this Word of the Kingdom shall be taught in all the world for a witness unto all nations and then shall the end come.

These are the future 7-Year Peace Plan believers, and the book of Acts will be re-lived at that time. They will receive the Latter Rain of Yahweh's Spirit when the truth is taught to every person on earth at that time. This has been Satan's world before that time comes all the way back to the 11 persecutions of the Roman Empire that killed off all the elect back then.

Ephesians 4:6,7,8; 11-16

6. One Yahweh and Father of all, who is above all, and through all, <u>and in you all</u>.

7. But unto every one of us is given the Spirit according to the measure of the gift of Yahweh.

8. Wherefore He saith, When He ascended up on high, He led captivity captive and gave gifts unto men.

11. And He gave some apostles [the original 12 disciples]; and some, prophets; [those who Yahweh spoke through] and some, evangelists [those who evangelize]; and some, shepherds [those who personally care for the sheep] and teachers [those who taught or gave instruction];

12. <u>For the perfecting of the believers, for the work of the ministry, for the edifying of the body of Yahweh:</u>

13. <u>Till we all come in the unity of the Faith, and of the knowledge of the Son of Yahweh</u>, unto <u>a perfect man, unto the measure of the stature of the fulness of Yahweh:</u>

14. <u>That we henceforth be no more children, tossed to and fro, and carried about with every wind of doctrine, by the sleight of men, and cunning craftiness, whereby they lie in wait to deceive;</u>

15. But speaking the truth in love, may grow up into Him in all things, which is the head, even Yahweh:

16. From whom the whole body fitly joined together and compacted by that which every joint supplieth, according to the effectual working in the measure of every part, maketh increase of the body unto the edifying of itself in love.

<u>In other words, when you first believe, you become a believer, but you are not Spirit-filled yet. So, the Spirit-filled believers were the ones who taught the new believers in Yahweh Messiah until Yahweh saw fit to fill them with His Spirit. The Spirit-filled people were taught by the Spirit and knew all things. The believers who were not Spirit-filled had to be taught of Yahweh's ways.</u>

Salvation is when you are filled with Yahweh's Spirit and not before.

They did not have salvation when they asked for forgiveness or when they were baptized in His Name, Yahweh. So, they were not so-called saved at that time.

Let me explain what the scriptures really teach: At the time of repentance, asking for forgiveness of transgressions is the first step to salvation. The person became an Apprentice for the infilling of Yahweh's Spirit, and Yahweh started helping them clean themselves up; at baptism, this was the second step to salvation, and they became a Candidate for the infilling of Yahweh's Spirit. This is when the person was thriving to serve Yahweh and Yahweh is still helping them to clean themselves up, so His Spirit can dwell in them. When this was done, they become a Journeyman, which was the third and last step to believing, and that is when the Master Yahweh filled the people with His Spirit, and this was a true believer in Yahweh.

Acts 5:32 And we are His witnesses of these things; and so is also <u>the Spirit, whom Yahweh hath given to them that obey Him.</u>

John 7:39 (*<u>But this spake he of the Spirit, which they that believed on him should receive</u>* for the Spirit was not yet given; because Immanuel was not yet esteemed.

Acts 1:8 But ye shall receive power, after that the Spirit comes upon you: and ye shall be witnesses unto me both in Jerusalem, and in all Judaea, and in Samaria, and unto the uttermost part of the earth.

Hosea 6:3 Then shall we know, if we follow on to know Yahweh: his going forth is prepared as the morning; and he shall come unto us as the rain, as the latter and former rain unto the earth.

Those from Pentecost to the last of the 11 Roman Emperor Persecutions received the Former Rain of Yahweh's Spirit infilling. The future 7-Year Peace Plan elect will receive the Latter Rain of Yahweh's Spirit infilling.

Hebrews 2:3,4

3. How shall we escape, if we neglect so great salvation; which at the first began to be spoken by the Master and was confirmed unto us by them that heard him.

4. Yahweh also bearing them witness, both with signs and wonders, and with diver's miracles, and gifts of the Spirit, according to His own will?

Luke 10:19 Behold, I give unto you power to tread on serpents and scorpions, and over all the power of the enemy: and nothing shall by any means hurt you.

NOTE: As you should be able to see Christians do not have Yahweh's Spirit nor do the so-called Pentecostals, as a matter of fact, no one today has Yahweh's Spirit infilling.

Romans 8:9 But ye are not in the flesh but in the Spirit, if so be the Spirit of Yahweh dwells in you. Now if any man has not the Spirit of Yahweh, he is none of His.

2 Corinthians 13:5 Examine yourselves, whether ye be in the faith; prove your own selves. Know ye not your own selves, how that Yahweh Messiah is in you, except ye be reprobates?

Now watch: If you are alive during the 7-Year Peace Plan, you will hear the whole truth and can believe it or not. This will lead to tribulation of the persecutions and killings of the elect. That is another reason you MUST have Yahweh's Spirit infilling for salvation, too.

How about us today? If you die before the 7-Year Peace Treaty, Yahweh will raise you up during the Millennial Kingdom and teach you Himself, but there will be no salvation at that time for those who are taught by Him. WHY? Because there will be no more excuses for when Satan is raised from the grave, who Yahweh will have killed at His coming. Satan will be given one last chance to deceive the world. Those people lived in Satan's world and then lived in Yahweh's Kingdom taught by Yahweh Himself, so they must be tried like in the days of Peter and Paul, and the coming Tribulation Period of the elect as they were tried and tested will also be tried and tested. So, they have a choice to believe in Yahweh, which is life, or Satan, which is death. This is the final battle of judgment.

Daniel 7:25 And he shall speak great words against Yahweh, and shall wear out the Elect of Yahweh, and think to change times and laws: and they shall be given into his hand until a time and times and the dividing of time.

The Elect during the last 3 1/2-year Tribulation Period and the last 3 1/2 years of the 7-Year Peace Plan will be given into the Pope's hand at this time.

CHAPTER 38

HOMOSEXUALITY:

Genesis 1:27-28

27: So Yahweh created man in his own image, in the image of Yahweh created he him; **male and female created he them**.

Remember, Yahweh created Adam and Eve, not Adam and Steve or Mary and Sherry.

28: And Yahweh blessed them, and Yahweh said unto them, **Be fruitful, and multiply, and replenish the earth**, Be fruitful, and multiply, and subdue it: and have dominion over the fish of the sea, and over the fowl of the air, and over every living thing that moveth upon the earth.

Nature itself tells us that two things of the same sex cannot reproduce. So homosexuals cannot be fruitful and multiply or replenish the earth.

Genesis 2:24

24: Therefore shall a man **leave his father and his mother, and shall cleave unto his wife**: and they shall be one flesh.

As we know, a **Mother** is a **female parent**.

Father is a **male parent**.

What is a male? Sex that fertilizes and begets offspring.

What is a female? Sex that bears offspring (woman or girl: feminine).

What is a man? An adult male person.

What is a woman? An adult female human being.

What is married? Being a husband or wife.

What is a husband? A married man.

What is a wife? A married woman.

What is a widower? A man whose wife has died and who has not remarried.

What is a widow? A woman whose husband has died and who has not remarried.

As you can see, Yahweh's plan has nothing to do with same-sex relationships, gays and lesbians, or homosexuals. When you speak of homosexuals, you speak of same-sex relationships, so for a homosexual to be able to reproduce, they must leave the same-sex relationship and come over to how it was meant to be. This is where the term BISEXUAL comes from, which is usually how homosexual diseases are transmitted to heterosexuals.

<u>Homosexual</u>: *One who is sexually attracted to the SAME sex.*

<u>Bisexual</u>: *One who is sexually attracted to BOTH sexes.*

<u>Heterosexual</u>: *One who is sexually attracted to the OPPOSITE sex. (The way Yahweh created man to be.)*

1 Kings 14:24

24. And there were also sodomites in the land, and they did according to all the abominations of the nations which Yahweh cast out before the children of Israel. ...

Leviticus 20:13

13. If a man also lie with mankind, as he lieth with a woman, both of them have committed an abomination: they shall surely be put to death; their blood shall be upon them.

Judaea was told by Yahweh to kill homosexuals so none would be found among them. Today, society is teaching the acceptance of them, but it will not change our Creator's mind. His death penalty for them is the Lake of Fire. Why were they to kill homosexuals? Homosexuality is a cancer to society.

Leviticus 18:22-30

22: **Thou shalt not lie with mankind, as with womankind: it is an abomination.**

23: Neither shalt thou lie with any beast to defile thyself therewith: neither shall any woman stand before a beast to lie down thereto: it is confusion.

24: **Defile not ye yourselves in any of these things: for in all these the nations are defiled which I cast out before you.**

25: **And the land is defiled: therefore I do visit the iniquity thereof upon it, and the land itself vomiteth out her inhabitants.**

26: Ye shall therefore keep my statutes and my judgments, and **shall not commit any of these abominations**; neither any of your own nation, nor any stranger that sojourneth among you:

27: **For all these abominations have the men of the land done, which were before you, and the land is defiled;**

As you can see, nations were destroyed for this perversion. No wonder gentiles were considered dogs.

28: That the land spew not you out also, when ye defile it, as it spewed out the nations that were before you.

29: **For whosoever shall commit any of these abominations, even the souls that commit them shall be cut off from among their people.**

30: Therefore shall ye keep mine ordinance, **that ye commit not any one of these abominable customs, which were committed before you, and that ye defile not yourselves therein**: I am Yahweh your Mighty One.

Genesis 19:4-8, 12-13, 24-25

4: But before they lay down, the men of the city, even the men of Sodom, compassed the house round, both old and young, all the people from every quarter:

5: And they called unto Lot, and said unto him, Where are the men which came into thee this night: bring them out unto us, that we may know them.

6: And Lot went out at the door unto them, and shut the door after him,

7: And said, I pray you, brethren, do not so wickedly.

8: Behold now, I have two daughters which have not known man; let me, I pray you, bring them out unto you, and do ye to them as is good in your eyes: only unto these men do nothing; for therefore came they under the shadow of my roof.

Lot was going to give these men his own two daughters to do with as they pleased so these men would not force their perverted homosexual acts upon his visitors.

12: And the man said unto Lot, Hast thou here any besides? Son-in-law, and thy sons, and thy daughters, and whatsoever thou has in the city, bring them out of this place:

13: **For we will destroy this place, because the cry of them is waxen great before the face of Yahweh and Yahweh hath sent us to destroy it.**

24: Then Yahweh rained upon Sodom and upon Gomorrah brimstone and fire from Yahweh out of heaven.

25: And he overthrew those cities, and all the plain, and all the inhabitants of the cities, and that which grew upon the ground.

Matthew 19:1-8

1 And it came to pass, that when Immanuel had finished these sayings, he departed from Galilee, and came into the coasts of Judaea beyond Jordan;

2 And great multitudes followed him; and he healed them there.

3 The Pharisees also came unto him, tempting him, and saying unto him, Is it lawful for a man to put away his wife for every cause?

4 And he answered and said unto them, Have ye not read, that he which made them at the beginning made them male and female,

5 And said, For this cause shall a man leave father and mother, and shall cleave to his wife: and they twain shall be one flesh?

6 Wherefore they are no more twain, but one flesh. What therefore Yahweh hath joined together, let not man put asunder.

Ephesians 5:3-7

3 But fornication, and all uncleanness, or covetousness, let it not be once named among you, as becometh Elect;

4 Neither filthiness, nor foolish talking, nor jesting, which are not convenient: but rather giving of thanks.

5 For this ye know, that no whoremonger, nor unclean person, nor covetous man, who is an idolater, hath any inheritance in the kingdom of the Messiah and of Yahweh.

6 Let no man deceive you with vain words: for because of these things cometh the wrath of Yahweh upon the children of disobedience.

7 Be not ye therefore partakers with them.

Colossians 3:5-7

5 Mortify therefore your members which are upon the earth; fornication, uncleanness, inordinate affection, evil concupiscence, and covetousness, which is idolatry:

6 For which things' sake the wrath of Yahweh cometh on the children of disobedience:

7 In the which ye also walked some time, when ye lived in them.

1 Timothy 1:10

10 For whoremongers, for them that defile themselves with mankind, for menstealers, for liars, for perjured persons, and if there be any other thing that is contrary to sound doctrine;

Titus 1:16

16 They profess that they know Yahweh; but in works they deny him, being abominable, and disobedient, and unto every good work reprobate.

Revelation 21:27

27 And there shall in no wise enter into it anything that defileth, neither whatsoever worketh abomination, or maketh a lie: but they which are written in the Lamb's book of life.

Romans 18:24-32

24: **Wherefore Yahweh also gave them up to uncleanness through the lusts of their own hearts, to dishonor their own bodies between themselves:**

25: Who changed the truth of Yahweh unto a lie and worshipped and served the creature more than the Creator, who is blessed forever.

26: **For this cause Yahweh gave them up unto vile affections: for even their women did change the natural use into that which is against nature.**

27: **And likewise, also the men, leaving the natural use of the woman, burned in their lust one toward another; men with men working that which is unseemly, and receiving in themselves that recompense of their error which as meet.**

28: **And even as they did not like to retain Yahweh in their knowledge, Yahweh gave them over to a reprobate mind, to do those things which are not convenient;**

29: Being filled with all unrighteousness, fornication, wickedness, covetousness, maliciousness; full of envy, murder, debate, deceit, malignity, whisperers,

30: Backbiters, haters of Yahweh, despiteful, proud, boasters, inventors of evil things, disobedient to parents,

31: **Without understanding, covenant breakers, without natural affection, implacable, unmerciful:**

32: **Who knowing the judgment of Yahweh, that they which commit such things are worthy of death, not only do the same, but have pleasure in them that do them.**

1 Cor. 6:9-10

9: **Know ye not that the unrighteous shall not inherit the kingdom of Yahweh? Be not deceived: neither fornicators, nor idolaters, nor adulterers, nor effeminate *(homosexuals)*, nor abusers of themselves with mankind.**

10: **Nor thieves, nor covetous, nor drunkards, nor revilers, nor extortioners, shall inherit the kingdom of Yahweh.**

11: And such WERE some of you; but ye are washed, but ye are sanctified, but ye are justified in the name of Yahweh, and by the Spirit of Yahweh.

Yes, there is hope for those who want to find the truth of it all and change their lives the way Yahweh meant it to be.

America and this world are becoming more accepting of perversion daily, and our own government now tries to force people to accept this perversion by calling it civil rights. It has come to the point where males saying they are females are now allowed in girls' sports and in their locker rooms. This is a Satanic Agenda pushed on mankind by liberal governments.

Whatever some people believe the Scriptures seem to say about homosexuality, they must not use that belief to deny homosexuals their basic civil rights. To discriminate against sexual or gender minorities is unjust and un-American.

Homosexuals have already penetrated our Boy and Girl Scout Organizations and our schools as teachers. Your children are being taught in schools about Sam and Dan, Mary and Sherry, homosexual couples as same-sex parents, and brainwashing the children of today. They are now actually teaching kids how to be homosexual in our schools. Homosexuality is now running rampant in our schools among teenagers. Homosexuals (lesbians) are now having artificial insemination so they can have children. The United States allows homosexuals to adopt children and allows homosexual marriages. This way, they can stay true to their homosexuality.

Pope John Paul II told homosexuals to come out of the closet, and it has gone from equal rights and the above to brainwashing young children to have sex changes, and the government does nothing to stop it. You can only imagine what the future generations will be like if Yahweh does not return to kill Satan and all the wicked with him; after all, this is totally Satan's world, and he knows his time is short.

All this should prove what Christianity really is, that it is of Satan.

You, as a people, you as nations, must turn back to Yahweh and stand up for the truth so your children can come out of the pit that you have and are putting them in. As the saying goes, If you don't stand for something, then you will fall for anything.

Homosexuals must turn away from their perverted lifestyle and turn to Yahweh, who shall set them free or have the same end as Sodom and Gomorrah when salvation is given again at the end of WW3.

<u>Yahweh's Warning</u>: *Jude verse 77: Even as Sodom and Gomorrah, and the cities about them in like manner, giving themselves over to fornication, and going after strange flesh, are set forth for an example, suffering the vengeance of eternal fire. I think the United States had better heed the warning of JUDE 7 before she, like Napoleon, meets her Waterloo.*

When Clinton was President, he legalized homosexuals to be in the military. What will be the long-term effect? How about the AIDS epidemic in our military? What about the morale of our heterosexual soldiers? Will someday our V.A. hospitals be filled with AIDS patients instead of the hurt and wounded? These are just some of the questions without answers yet.

Leviticus 18:24-25

24: Defile not ye yourselves in any of these things: for in all these the nations are defiled which I cast out before you.

25: And the land is defiled: therefore, I do visit the iniquity thereof upon it, and the land itself vomited out her inhabitants.

The United States is condoning what Yahweh condemns, things like:

HOMOSEXUAL MARRIAGES (man with man, women with women).

You can see now what direction the United States is headed, calling bad good. What does Yahweh say about this?

ISAIAH 5:20-21; 21. Woe to them that call evil good, and good evil; that put darkness for light, and light for darkness, that put bitter for sweet, and sweet for bitter! 21. Woe to them that are wise in their own eyes, and prudent in their own sight!

The United States is following the world's lead, and politicians today will lay hold of liberal agendas to gain votes in their greed for power. The United States is slowly self-destructing and doesn't realize it. It is already another Sodom and Gomorrah.

Yahweh would have to apologize for the destruction of Sodom and Gomorrah (Which was set forth as an example, Jude verse 7) if destruction is not brought upon the United States and the world and will in Judgement.

Romans 1:24-32

24. Wherefore Yahweh also gave them up to uncleanness through the lusts of their own hearts, to dishonor their own bodies between themselves:

25. Who changed the truth of Yahweh into a lie and worshiped and served the creature more than the Creator, who is blessed forever.

26. For this cause Yahweh gave them up unto vile affections: for even their women did change the natural use into that which is against nature:

27. And likewise also the men, leaving the natural use of the woman, burned in their lust one toward another; men with men working that which is unseemly, and receiving in themselves that recompense of their error which was meet.

28. And even as they did not like to retain Yahweh in their knowledge, Yahweh gave them over to a reprobate mind, to do those things which are not convenient;

29. Being filled with all unrighteousness, fornication, wickedness, covetousness, maliciousness; full of envy, murder, debate, deceit, malignity; whisperers,

30. Backbiters, haters of Yahweh, despiteful, proud, boasters, inventors of evil things, disobedient to parents,

31. Without understanding, covenant breakers, without natural affection, implacable, unmerciful:

32. Who knowing the JUDGMENT OF YAHWEH, that they which commit such things are worthy of death, not only do the same, but have pleasure in them that do them.

In the 1950s, Psychiatry still regarded homosexuality as a psychological and not biological problem. Moreover, it was classified as a sexual perversion, a treatable disease that could be cured through appropriate treatment. However, powerful dark forces desired this otherwise. They worked to promote the Homosexual Agenda by encouraging activists to publicly protest their conviction that homosexuality was not only natural and somehow noble but also a preferable way of life.

HOMOSEXUALITY IS A FORM OF BIRTH CONTROL

Not only is our government trying to get rid of morality in this country, but they are using different things to help stop future population growth; besides the pill, another one is abortion, and then there is homosexuality. Why do I say this? During the Greek Empire, homosexuality was big, especially with the Olympians. Then the Roman Empire took over, and they have seen a big problem with it. The problem was homosexuals could not make babies to supply the Roman army with soldiers, so they put a stop to it.

WAKE UP, AMERICA, WAKE UP, WORLD, DON'T BE BRAINWASHED!

THE TERM GAY:

"The term was originally used to refer to feelings of being "carefree," "happy," or "bright and showy;" it had also come to acquire some connotations of "immorality" as early as 1637. The term's use as a reference to homosexuality may date as early as the late 19th century, but its use gradually increased in the 20th century. In modern English, gay has come to be used as an adjective and as a noun, referring to the people, especially men, and the practices and cultures associated with homosexuality. By the end of the 20th century, the word gay was recommended by major LGBT groups and style guides to describe people attracted to members of the same sex."

CHAPTER 39

GREED

¹⁷ This I say therefore, and testify in Yahweh, that ye henceforth walk not as other Gentiles walk, in the vanity of their mind,

¹⁸ Having the understanding darkened, being alienated from the life of Yahweh through the ignorance that is in them, because of the blindness of their heart:

¹⁹ Who being past feeling have given themselves over unto lasciviousness, to work all uncleanness with greediness.

²⁰ But ye have not so learned Immanuel;

²¹ If so, be that ye have heard him, and have been taught by him, as the truth is in Immanuel:

²² That ye put off concerning the former conversation the old man, which is corrupt according to the deceitful lusts;

²³ And be renewed in the spirit of your mind;

²⁴ And that ye put on the new man, which after Yahweh is created in righteousness. (and true holiness) <-- was added to that verse!

Mark 4:19

The cares of this world, the deceitfulness of riches, and the desires for other things enter in and choke the word, and it becomes unfruitful.

He also that received seed among the thorns is he that heareth the word; and the care of this world, and the deceitfulness of riches, choke the word, and he becometh unfruitful.

Luke 8:14

And that which fell among thorns are they, which, when they have heard, go forth, and are choked with cares and riches and pleasures of this life, and bring no fruit to perfection.

Luke 3:14

And the soldiers likewise demanded of him, saying, And what shall we do? And he said unto them, Do violence to no man, neither accuse any falsely; and be content with your wages.

Luke 12:15-21

[15] And he said unto them, Take heed, and beware of covetousness: for a man's life consisteth not in the abundance of the things which he possesseth.

[16] And he spake a parable unto them, saying, The ground of a certain rich man brought forth plentifully:

[17] And he thought within himself, saying, What shall I do, because I have no room where to bestow my fruits?

[18] And he said, This will I do: I will pull down my barns, and build greater; and there will I bestow all my fruits and my goods.

[19] And I will say to my soul, Soul, thou hast much goods laid up for many years; take thine ease, eat, drink, and be merry.

20 But Yahweh said unto him, thou fool, this night thy soul shall be required of thee: then whose shall those things be, which thou hast provided?

21 So is he that layeth up treasure for himself, and is not rich toward Yahweh.

Luke 6:24-25

24 But woe unto you that are rich! for ye have received your consolation.

25 Woe unto you that are full! for ye shall hunger. Woe unto you that laugh now! for ye shall mourn and weep.

Luke 16: 11-13

11 If therefore ye have not been faithful in the unrighteous mammon, who will commit to your trust the true riches?

12 And if ye have not been faithful in that which is another man's, who shall give you that which is your own?

13 No servant can serve two masters: for either he will hate the one and love the other; or else he will hold to the one and despise the other. Ye cannot serve Yahweh and mammon.

Ephesians 4:28

Let him that stole steal no more: but rather let him labour, working with his hands the thing which is good, that he may have to give to him that needeth.

Proverbs 1:19

So are the ways of every one that is greedy of gain; which taketh away the life of the owners thereof.

Proverbs 13:2

A man shall eat good by the fruit of his mouth: but the soul of the transgressors shall eat violence.

Proverbs 14:23

In all labour there is profit: but the talk of the lips tendeth only to penury.

Proverbs 15:27

He that is greedy of gain troubleth his own house; but he that hateth gifts shall live.

Job 31:24-25,29

24 If I have made gold my hope, or have said to the fine gold, Thou art my confidence;

25 If I rejoice because my wealth was great, and because mine hand had gotten much.

29 If I have rejoiced at the ruin of him who hated me, or exulted when evil overtook him

Proverbs 21: 16, 25-26, 28

16 The man that wandereth out of the way of understanding shall remain in the congregation of the dead.

25 The desire of the slothful killeth him; for his hands refuse to labour.

26 He coveteth greedily all the day long: but the righteous giveth and spareth not.

28 This also were an iniquity to be punished by the judge, for I should have denied the Yahweh that is above.

Isaiah 56:11

Yea, they are greedy dogs which can never have enough, and they are shepherds that cannot understand: they all look to their own way, everyone for his gain, from his quarter.

Jeremiah 17:10-11

10 I Yahweh search the heart, I try the reins, even to give every man according to his ways, and according to the fruit of his doings.

11 As the partridge sitteth on eggs, and hatcheth them not; so, he that getteth riches, and not by right, shall leave them in the midst of his days, and at his end shall be a fool.

GAMBLING OF ANY KIND, STEALING, COVETOUSNESS, RICHES MAN'S WAY VS YAHWEH'S WAY.

CHAPTER 40

JOSEPH AND MARIAM TOOK A BOAT TO EGYPT

FROM A PORT AT ZEBULON'S SEACOAST.

THEY DID NOT WALK OVER A THOUSAND MILES AS SOME SAY, WITH A TODDLER TO EGYPT.

EACH OF THE 12 TRIBES HAD A FAMILY BANNER AND ZEBULUN HAD A BOAT ON A WHITE BACKGROUND

Genesis 49:13 Zebulun shall dwell at the haven of the sea; and he shall be for a haven of ships; and his border shall be unto Zidon.

Haifa was a seaport city and where Joseph and Mariam most likely departed for Egypt from, for its proximity TO Bethlehem.

THEY SPENT 2 YEARS IN EGYPT; IMMANUEL WAS 4 YEARS OLD WHEN THEY LEFT.

On 6 August 1868, the founders of the Templers,[Templars were Catholics working for the Papacy. Christoph Hoffmann and Georg David Hardegg, their families and a group of fellow Templers, left Germany for Palestine, landing in HAIFA on 30 October. They had already come to the conclusion that basing themselves in Jerusalem wouldn't be practical, planning to settle nearby, close to Nazareth (WOULD THAT BE BETHLEHEM, OF COARSE? THE PROOF IS IN THE PUDDING.), but during their journey they were advised that Haifa would be more suitable, having a good harbor and climate. Hardegg stayed in Haifa, while Hoffmann moved on to establish other colonies. [Just so happened one was Bethlehem.]

THE FOLLOWING PROVES THAT BOATS WERE USED ALL THE TIME FOR TRANSPORTATION TO NAVIGATE LARGE BODIES OF WATER.

JOHN 6:22-25

22 The next day, the <u>people who were standing on the other side of the sea realized that no other boat had been there except the one His disciples had boarded, and that Immanuel had not boarded the boat with His disciples, but His disciples had gone away alone.</u>

23 <u>Then other boats came from Tiberias</u>, **near the place where they ate the bread after Immanuel had given thanks.**

24 **When the people therefore saw that Immanuel was not there, nor His disciples, <u>they also boarded the boats and came to Capernaum</u>, seeking Immanuel.**

25 And when they found Him on the other side of the sea, they said to Him, "Rabbi, when did You come here?"

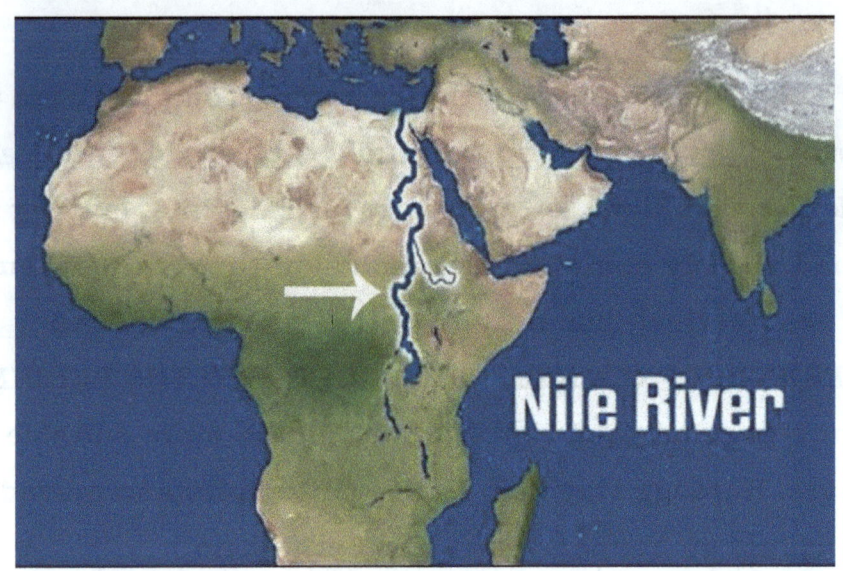

THIS MAP SHOWS HOW MUCH EASIER IT WAS TO TAKE A BOAT TO EGYPT FROM ZEBULON, WHICH TOOK IN THE COAST OF THE MEDITERANIAN SEA AND EXITED OUT AT ONE OF THE EGYPTIAN PORTS NEARER TO THEM. THEY DID NOT WALK ALL THAT WAY WITH A TODDLER. WHERE THEY ENDED UP IN EGYPT, NO ONE KNOWS. THAT WAS ACTUALLY THE SAFEST WAY TO GO TO EGYPT.

Genesis 49:13

Zebulun shall dwell at the haven of the sea, and he *shall be* **for an haven of ships, and his border** *shall be* **unto Zidon.**

The territory Zebulun was allocated was at the southern end of <u>the Galilee</u>, with its eastern border being the <u>Sea of Galilee</u>, the western border being the <u>Mediterranean Sea</u>, the south being bordered by the <u>Tribe of Issachar</u>, and the north by <u>Asher</u> on the western side and <u>Naphtali</u> on the eastern.

Deuteronomy 33:18-19

¹⁸ And of Zebulun he said, Rejoice, Zebulun, in thy going out; and, Issachar, in thy tents.

¹⁹ They shall call the people unto the mountain; there they shall offer offerings of righteousness: for **they shall suck of the abundance of the seas**, and of treasures hid in the sand.

GOODS FROM OTHER COUNTRIES ON SHIPS.

Genesis 49:13

ESV "Zebulun shall dwell at the shore of the sea; he shall become a haven for ships, and his border shall be at Sidon.

NIV "Zebulun will live by the seashore and become a haven for ships; his border will extend toward Sidon.

NASB 'Zebulun will reside at the seashore; and he *shall be* a harbor for ships, And his flank *shall be* toward Sidon.

CSB Zebulun will live by the seashore and will be a harbor for ships, and his territory will be next to Sidon.

NLT 'Zebulun will settle by the seashore and will be a harbor for ships; his borders will extend to Sidon.

KJV Zebulun shall dwell at the haven of the sea; and he shall be for an haven of ships; and his border shall be unto Zidon.

NKJV "Zebulun shall dwell by the haven of the sea; He *shall become* a haven for ships, and his border shall adjoin Sidon.

The third lot came up for Zebulun, clan by clan: The boundary of their inheritance went as far as Sarid. Going west, it ran to Maralah, touched Dabbesheth, and extended to the ravine near Jokneam. It turned east from Sarid toward the sunrise to the territory of Kisloth Tabor and went on to Daberath and up to Japhia. Then it continued eastward to Gath Hepher and Eth Kazin; it came out at Rimmon and turned toward Neah. **There the boundary went around on the north to Hannathon and ended at the Valley of Iphtah El. Included were Kattath, Nahalal, Shimron, Idalah and Bethlehem.** There were twelve towns and their villages. These towns and their villages were the inheritance of Zebulun, clan by clan. (Jos 19:10-16).

CHAPTER 41

THE OLIVET DISCOURSE ON BOTH TRIBULATION PERIODS

Matthew 24:9-14

9 You: and ye shall be hated of all nations for my name's sake.

THE NAME HATED WAS YAHWEH, 5th seal; the ELECT WERE ALL KILLED OFF and are all dead.

10 And then shall many be offended, and shall betray one another, and shall hate one another. Tribulation back then.

Great falling Away.

11 And **many false prophets shall rise, and shall deceive many.**

THE FALSE PROPHETS ROSE UP AFTER THE FIRST TRIBULATION THEY CANNOT ARISE AFTER THE SECOND TRIBULATION PERIOD; IT IS ONLY 3 ½ YEARS AND EVERYONE WILL BE TAKEN OR BURNED UP.

12 And because **iniquity shall abound, the love of many shall wax cold.**

13 **But he that shall endure unto the end, the same shall be saved.**

14 And this Word of **the kingdom shall be taught in all the world** for a witness unto all nations; and then shall the end come. **<-- proof Paul proved it was, for those back then, it was the end.**

Matthew 24:21 — The New King James Version (NKJV)

21 For **then there will be great tribulation, such as has not been since the beginning of the world until this time, no, nor ever shall be.** (TRIBULATION BACK THEN)

Matthew 24:6

6 And **ye shall hear of wars and rumors of wars**: see that ye **be not troubled**: for **all these things must come to pass, but the end is not yet**.

THE 11 ROMAN EMPEROR PERSECUTIONS BACK THEN LASTED 256 YEARS, THEIR TRIBULATION PERIOD. IN VERSE 6, THE FUTURE TRIBULATION LASTS ONLY 3 ½ YEARS, AND HIS RETURN IS DURING THE ARMAGEDDON WAR, SO IT WAS WRITTEN FOR THOSE BACK THEN.

Psalms 2:1-6

1 **Why do the heathen rage, and the people imagine a vain thing?**

2 **The kings of the earth set themselves, and the rulers take counsel together, against Yahweh, and against his anointed,** *saying*,

3 **Let us break their bands asunder, and cast away their cords from us**.

4 **He that sitteth in the heavens shall laugh: Yahweh shall have them in derision.**

This happened with the first Tribulation Period and will happen again with the last Tribulation Period.

5 **Then shall he speak unto them in his wrath, and vex them in his sore displeasure**

6 Yet have I set my king upon my holy hill of Zion.

This happened with the first Tribulation Period, why there were 11 separate Persecutions and will happen again with the last Tribulation, with the Papacy and 10 World Union leaders.

Mark 13:13 — The New King James Version (NKJV)

13 And **you will be hated by all for My name's sake**. But **he who endures to the end shall be saved.**

Luke 21:19 — The New King James Version (NKJV)

19 By your patience possess your souls.

Matthew 24:22 — English Standard Version (ESV)

22 And **if those days had not been cut short, no human being would be saved**. But for the sake of the elect those days will be cut short.

FOR THE LAST TRIBULATION PERIOD.

Mark 13:20 — The New King James Version (NKJV)

20 And **unless Yahweh had shortened those days, no flesh would be saved; but for the elect's sake, whom He chose, He shortened the days.**

Luke 21:24 —KJ

And **they shall fall by the edge of the sword** and shall be **led away captive into all nations:** and ZION shall be trodden down of the Gentiles, **until the times of the Gentiles be fulfilled.**

The "times of the Gentiles" end at Yahweh's return.

CHAPTER 42

HOW THE MESSIAH FULFILLED THE SPRING FEAST

SPRING FEASTS:

FEAST OF PASSOVER - Became the offered Lamb.

FEAST OF UNLEAVENED BREAD - Was buried - the last supper, "This is my body."

7th Day Sabbath - He was resurrected. The First day after his 7th-day resurrection was the Feast of First Fruits.

FEAST OF FIRST FRUITS - He was the priest who offered unto the Father the First Fruits of his wave offering of the 144,000 babies that Herod had killed, the first fruits.

FEAST OF PENTECOST - <u>50 days after the Feast of First Fruits came to Pentecost, which was fulfilled with the outpouring of His Spirit.</u>

The 3 fall Feasts that are not fulfilled yet, which he will fulfill at His return.

FALL FEASTS:

I BELIEVE YAHWEH MESSIAH WILL RETURN DURING THE FEAST OF TRUMPETS DURING THE ARMAGEDDON WAR AT THE VERY END OF THE TRIBULATION PERIOD.

YOU WON'T KNOW THE DAY OR HOUR.

Matthew 25:13

13 "Watch therefore, for ye know neither the day nor the hour wherein the Son of man cometh."

YOU WILL KNOW ABOUT WHEN IT WILL HAPPEN. HE COMES DURING THE ARMAGEDDON WAR. NO ONE KNOWS WHEN THAT WILL BE.

Luke 21:28

28 And when these things begin to come to pass, then look up, and lift up your heads; for your redemption draweth nigh.

The **Feast of Trumpets**, also known as **Rosh Hashanah**, occurs on **Tishri 1, the first month of the Hebrew civil year. Rosh Hashanah is a** New Year celebration in Judaea.

Rosh Hashanah means "head of the year," referring to the day of the New Year. Hebrew Civil Calendar.

How fitting He was born on Yahweh's New Year, Nissan 1 on the moon calendar, to keep track of the new moons for each new month. Then returns on the Feast of Trumpets, ten days of consecration and repentance before Yahweh, one of those days, the 7th and last Trump is blown to announce his coming. Since he was born on the 1st of the New Year, is it feasible that he will also return on the 1st of the Hebrew New Year, it remains to be seen.

Yom Teruah, or the Feast of Trumpets, is on the 1st through the 10th of the month; on the first day of it is the blowing of the ram's horn, the shofa**, Yom Kippur is on the 10th, and Sukkot is on the 15th.** *This is a full month of celebrations.*

Yom Teruah - Feast of Trumpets

Leviticus 23:23-25

23 And Yahweh spake unto Moses, saying,

24 Speak unto the children of Judaea, saying, <u>In the seventh month, in the first day of the month, shall ye have a Sabbath, a memorial of blowing of trumpets, a righteous convocation.</u>

25 Ye shall do no servile work therein: but ye shall offer an offering made by fire unto Yahweh.

<u>Feast of Trumpets starts on a full moon.</u>

Matthew 24:29-31

29 Immediately after the tribulation of those days shall the sun be darkened, and the moon shall not give her light, and the stars shall fall from heaven, and the powers of the heavens shall be shaken.

30 And then shall appear the sign of the Son of man in heaven: and then shall all the tribes of the earth mourn, and they shall see the Son of man coming in the clouds of heaven with power and great honor.

31 And he shall send his Messengers with a great sound of a trumpet, and they shall gather together his elect from the four winds, from one end of heaven to the other.

1 Corinthians 15:51-53

51 Behold, I shew you a mystery; We shall not all sleep, but we shall all be changed.

52 In a moment, in the twinkling of an eye, at the last trump: for the trumpet shall sound, and the dead shall be raised incorruptible, and we shall be changed.

1 Thessalonians 3:16 For <u>Yahweh Himself shall descend from heaven with a shout, with the voice of the arch-messenger, and with the trump of Yahweh</u>: and the dead in Yahweh shall rise first.

SEE HOW HE COULD NOT HAVE BEEN BORN DURING THE FEAST OF TRUMPETS?

<u>Yom Kippur</u> - Feast of Atonement / Judgment - Noah and the coming back of Yahweh compared.

A. Noah was warned 7 days before the flood came:

This last generation will be warned 7 years before his coming with the Papacy's 7-Year Peace Plan.

Genesis 7:4

<u>For yet seven days,</u> and I will cause it to rain upon the earth forty days and forty nights, and every living substance that I have made will I destroy from off the face of the earth.

A. People are warned 7 Years before Yahweh returns; 7-Year Peace Treaty:

Daniel 9:27

And <u>he shall confirm the covenant with many for one week</u>: and in the midst of the week, he shall cause the offerings to cease, and for the overspreading of abominations he shall make it desolate, even until the consummation, and that determined shall be poured upon the desolate.

B. Noah takes all those who are going to be saved from the flood onto the Ark:

Genesis 7:13

In the selfsame day entered Noah, and Shem, and Ham, and Japheth, the sons of Noah, and Noah's wife, and the three wives of his sons with them, into the ark.

B. Yahweh takes all those who are going to be saved into spacecraft:

1 Thessalonians 4:16-17

16 For Yahweh Himself shall descend from heaven with a shout, with the voice of the arch-messenger, and with the trump of Yahweh: and the dead in Yahweh Messiah shall rise first

17 Then we which are alive and remain shall be (caught up together with them in the clouds,) to meet Yahweh in the air; and so shall we ever be with Yahweh.

C. Noah's Ark raised them up above the wicked that were killed:

Genesis 7:18

And the waters prevailed and were increased greatly upon the earth; and the ark went upon the face of the waters.

The wicked were killed off.

C. Yahweh's spacecraft raises His Elect above those that are killed.

Luke 16:26

"And beside all this, between us and you there is a great gulf fixed: so that they which would pass from hence to you cannot; neither can they pass to us, that would come from thence."

The Wicked were killed off.

D. Noah's Ark came down on Mount Ararat:

Genesis 8:4

And the ark rested in the seventh month, on the seventeenth day of the month, upon the mountains of Ararat.

D. Yahweh's spacecraft comes down on Mount of Olives:

Zechariah 14:4

And his feet shall stand in that day upon the mount of Olives, which is before Zion on the east, and the mount of Olives shall cleave in the midst thereof toward the east and toward the west, and there shall be a very great valley; and half of the mountain shall remove toward the north, and half of it toward the south.

E. Noah's family re-populates the earth:

Genesis 9:1

And Yahweh blessed Noah and his sons, and said unto them, be fruitful, and multiply, and replenish the earth.

Isaiah 35:10

And the ransomed of Yahweh shall return and come to Zion with songs and everlasting joy upon their heads: they shall obtain joy and gladness, and sorrow and sighing shall flee away.

E. Those that never heard the truth will re-populate the earth:

Daniel 7:12

As concerning the rest of the beasts, they had their dominion taken away: (yet their lives were prolonged for a season and time.)

Jeremiah 16:19

"O Yahweh, my strength, and my fortress, and my refuge in the day of affliction, the Gentiles shall come unto thee from the ends of the earth, and shall say, surely our fathers have inherited lies, vanity, and things wherein there is no profit."

Jeremiah 3:17

At that time they will call Zion the throne of Yahweh and all nations will gather in Zion to honor the name of Yahweh. No longer will they follow the stubbornness of their evil hearts.

Revelation 22:14-15

14. Blessed are they that do his commandments, that they may have right to the tree of life and may enter in through the gates into the city.

15. For without are dogs, and sorcerers, and whoremongers, and murderers, and idolaters, and whosoever loveth and maketh a lie.

NOTE: Why are all those in verse 15 above without and cannot enter the gates of the city? Because these are those, who had never heard the whole truth and were raised from the dead after Yahweh's return to be taught by Yahweh himself the whole truth, that way there will be no excuses if they are deceived by Satan when he deceives the world one last time before the White Throne Judgement. They will serve Satan or Yahweh. Their choice, Yahweh, they will be filled with his Spirit, which gives salvation; those that serve Satan will be thrown into the Lake of Fire and never exist again.

This is another person that I had a remark from on Facebook:

Deborah Kolbaska Heins - I may have to chew the fat with you on this subject, Mr. Stanfield. I was very impressed with so many of your posts. Intelligent and insightful, however, you seem to have a tremendous distaste for Christianity. Why so much?

I believe I told her.

Well, my brother has a PhD in Divinity and Church History. You and he could have quite a debate, I'm sure.

Yahweh's truth stands strong against Christian beliefs. AS A MATTER OF FACT, YAHWEH'S TRUTH BLOWS CHRISTIANITY OUT OF THE WATER.

FINAL WORD: The elect in the days of the Apostles believed and read the inerrant Word of Yahweh, not what is called the Christian Word of God, the Bible, or the Scriptures that we have today. They are a lying deceit. Christianity and all world religions are all man-made and are of Satan. Christianity will absorb every one of them when Christianity becomes the religion of the world that will enforce the Mark of the Beast/Papacy with the symbol of Christianity, the Cross. Listen to this video; it proves what Christianity is, yet people will stay in the lie. They have no clue as to what road they need to find.

<u>After years of serving in her church, she thought she was saved until this happened...</u>

Copy the above and put it in your search the web to find it. Proves just how much people are brainwashed and think Christianity is the only hope for salvation.

CHAPTER 43

WHERE MAN ORIGINATED AT

MAN STARTED IN THE MIDDLE EAST, NOT AFRICA, AS SCIENTISTS TRY TO MAKE PEOPLE BELIEVE.

Let's go back to the beginning with Adam and Eve in the Garden of Eden, the beginning of mankind here on this earth. Where the people are being is considered the world. The Garden of Eden was the world at that time.

Where the Garden of Eden was located.

Genesis 2:8-14

Yahweh planted a garden toward the east, in Eden; and there He placed the man whom He had formed. Out of the ground Yahweh caused to grow every tree that is pleasing to the sight and good for food; the tree of life also in the midst of the garden, and the tree of the knowledge of good and evil. Now **a river flowed out of Eden to water the garden; and from there it divided and became four rivers. The name of the first is Pishon; it flows around the whole land of Havilah**, where there is gold. The gold of that land is good; the bdellium and the onyx stone are there. **The name of the second river is Gihon; it flows around the whole land of Cush.** The **name of the third river is Tigris; it flows east of Assyria**. And **the fourth river is the Euphrates**.

Compare this on the map, you can see they get the Euphrates and Tigris rivers right, but it seems no one can agree with the other two, the Pishon and Gihon rivers.

Abraham was born in Ur, in the Middle East, not Africa.

Egytian Empire 1450 B.C.E. Is not ruling the inhabited world.

- **Babylon (605-536 B.C.)**
- **Medo-Persia (536-330 B.C.)**
- **Greece (330–63 B.C.)**
- **Roman Empire Rome (63 B.C. – ongoing)**

Look at the main 4 empires, Babylonian, Medo-Persia, Grecian, and the Roman. Each one took over the populations of the world in their times as each empire progressed. People were migrating and were keeping up with the expanding of empires.

We are still living in the Roman Empire Era. Scriptures teach that the Roman Empire would be the last Empire on earth, which became the new form of government, the end-day Babylonian Religious Government System, before Yahweh returns and destroys it. Where the Pope's title replaced the title of Emperor. The Roman Empire ruled the inhabited world back then.

Revelation 17:10

And there are seven kings: five are fallen,

Nimrod was given the first Kingdom on earth. He lived during the 21st and 22nd centuries B.C.E. Nimrod built the City of Babylon, and it became the Capital City of the Babylonian Empire. Therefore, Nimrod is the rider on the White Horse in the First Seal of Revelation and represents the Babylonian Empire.

1. Egyptian EMPIRE - 16th century BC and the 11th century BC
2. Babylonian EMPIRE - 605-536 B.C. - <u>First Seal</u>
3. Assyrian EMPIRE- 900 - 607 B.C.
4. Medo - Persian EMPIRE - 536-330 B.C. – <u>Second Seal</u>
5. Grecian EMPIRE - 330–63 B.C. – <u>Third Seal</u>

and one is,

6. Roman EMPIRE - 63 B.C. – ongoing, C.E. – <u>Fourth Seal</u> - At the time of John's writing of Revelation.

7. Roman Empire - with a religious form of government – Papacy. – The <u>Fifth Seal is the rule of the Papacy. We are living at the very end of it now.</u> Revelation 13:12 Then I saw another beast (Papacy / Pope) coming up out of the earth; he had two horns like a lamb, but he sounded like a dragon. People were fleeing the Roman persecutions and the Papacy persecutions and they had plenty of room to run. Even up to this day, the Papacy is still working on its persecution of the peoples of the world. Satan is all about death and the grave, and history proves that fact.

8. ROMAN WORLD EMPIRE – Roman Religious Empire – Papacy, ruling from Zion.

WE ARE NOW SEEING THE COMEBACK OF THE POWER OF THE PAPACY. WE ARE LIVING AT THE VERY END OF THE FIFTH SEAL WHEN THE PAPACY IS ABOUT TO TAKE AND RULE THE WORLD FROM ZION. HE WAS, HE IS NOT BUT YET IS. Pope over Secular and Religious governments/ One World Government, One World Religion [Christianity] at the very end Tribulation Period.

Scriptures speak of the main 4 empires. Babylon, Medo-Persia, Grecian and Roman Empires. What is the significance of naming all 8 of these? They all ruled over Judaea throughout history. Number 8 is still the future.

WE ARE STILL LIVING IN THE ROMAN EMPIRE EVEN THOUGH THE POPE LOST HIS POWER WHEN NAPOLEAN CAPTURED HIM AND TOOK HIS POWER AWAY. WE ARE NOW SEEING THE COME BACK TO POWER OF THE POPE. WE ARE LIVING AT THE VERY END OF THE FIFTH SEAL WHEN THE PAPACY IS ABOUT TO TAKE AND RULE THE WORLD FROM ZION. HE WAS, HE IS NOT BUT YET IS. Pope over Secular and Religious governments/ One World Government, One World Religion [Christianity] at the very end Tribulation Period.

The 10 Toes are the last day Papacy 10 World Unions / 10 Kings who have no kingdom yet, that will give their power over to the Pope ruling from Zion.

NOW FOR THE WORLD CENSUS:

New American Standard Bible (NASB)

Luke 2:1 Now in those days a decree went out from Caesar Augustus, that A CENSUS BE TAKEN IN ALL THE INHABITED EARTH.

New Living Translation (NLT)

Luke 2:1.

At that time the Roman emperor, Augustus, decreed that A CENSUS SHOULD BE TAKEN THROUGHOUT THE ROMAN EMPIRE.

New Living Translation (NLTA)

Luke 2:1.

At that time the Roman emperor, Augustus, decreed that A CENSUS SHOULD BE TAKEN THROUGHOUT THE ROMAN EMPIRE.

Wycliffe Bible (WYC)

Luke 2:1

And it was done in those days, a commandment went out from the emperor Augustus [a commandment went out from Caesar Augustus], that all the world should be described.

World English Bible (WEB)

Luke 2:1

Now in those days, a decree went out from Caesar Augustus that all the world should be enrolled.

Young's Literal Translation (YLT)

Luke 2:1

And it came to pass in those days, there went forth <u>a decree from Caesar Augustus, that all the world be enrolled</u>.

Revised Standard Version Catholic Edition (RSVCE)

Luke 2:1

In those <u>days a decree went out from Caesar Augustus that all the world should be enrolled.</u>

New Revised Standard Version Catholic Edition (NRSVCE)

Luke 2:1

In those days <u>a decree went out from Emperor Augustus that all the world should be registered.</u>

Holman Christian Standard Bible (HCSB)

Luke 2:1

In those days a decree went out <u>from Caesar Augustus that the whole empire should be registered.</u>

1599 Geneva Bible (GNV)

Luke 2:1

And it came to pass in those days, that there **came a decree from Augustus Caesar, that all the world should be taxed.**

King James

Luke 2:1

And it came to pass in those days, that there went out **a decree from Caesar Augustus that ALL THE WORLD SHOULD BE TAXED.**

From the above verses, people should be able to see that the Roman Empire engulfed all the people that inhabited the earth at that time. Knowing this, you will now understand how they went to the ends of the world, the populated world.

Now for the preaching of Yahweh's Word to the WORLD!

Matthew 28:15

15. And he said unto them, **go ye into all the world, and teach the Word to every creature.**

Mark 16:15

Go ye into all the world, and teach the Word to every creature.

Matthew 28:19

Go ye, therefore, and teach all nations, baptizing them in the name of the Father, and of the Son, and of the Spirit. (Yahweh)

Mark 16:20

And **they went forth, and taught everywhere,** Yahweh working with them, and confirming the word with signs following.

Acts 8:4

Therefore **they that were scattered abroad went everywhere teaching the Word.**

Romans 1:5

By whom **we have received power and apostleship,** **for obedience to the faith among all nations**, for his name:

Romans 10:18

Their sound went into all the earth, and their words unto the ends of the world.

Acts 17:6

And when they found them not, they drew Jason and certain brethren unto the rulers of the city, crying, **these that have turned the world upside down** have come hither also;

Romans 1:8

First, I thank Yahweh through Yahweh Messiah for you all, **that your faith is spoken of throughout the whole world.**

Colossians 1: 5, 6

5. **Ye heard the Word of truth.**

6. **Which has come unto you, as it is in all the world.**

Luke 24:47-48

47. And **that repentance and remission of transgressions should be taught in His Name (Yahweh) among all nations, beginning at Zion.**

48. And **ye are witnesses of these things.**

Colossians 1:23

If ye continue in the faith grounded and settled, and be not moved away from the hope of the word, which ye have heard, and **which was taught to every creature which is under heaven; whereof I Paul am made a minister.**

Titus 2:11

For **the Word of Yahweh that brings salvation hath appeared to all men.**

(THAT HAPPENED BACK THEN AND WILL HAPPEN AGAIN IN THE FUTURE)

From the above verses, people should be able to see that the Roman Empire engulfed all the people on this earth at that time. The above verses are what brought about the 10 Roman Emperor persecutions that killed off the last of Yahweh Messiah's elect from Pentecost up to that time.

Revelation 6:8

And I looked, and behold a pale horse: and his name that sat on him was Death, and the grave followed with him (Satan). And **power was given unto them (Emperors) over the fourth part of the earth**, to kill with sword, and with hunger, and with death, and with the beasts of the earth.

People only inhabited just ¼ of the earth at that time.

The **PALE HORSE** represents **Death / Satan**

The Pale Horse rider is Death / Satan. (THEM) The Emperors of Rome.

Today, that is the Pope who sits under Saint Peter's Dome.

The Roman Empire killed Yahweh's people all off.

The kings of the earth stood up against Yahweh and his messiah.

Numerous scientific studies have proposed to have shown that a small group of individuals migrated out of eastern Africa and eventually expanded into most of today's populations. As shown from the migrating map, you can see people went into Africa not out from it in the beginning of populating the area. They teach that man's creation started in Africa, but this is not true, and all the above proves that it is a lie. Man was created in the Middle East, where the Garden of Eden was located, and they spread out from that area.

A team led by Professor Lee Berger, a palaeoanthropologist from the University of the Witwatersrand in Johannesburg, found two well-preserved skeletons of a human ancestor species that has never before been seen. Berger and his team described the new hominid and named it *Australopithecus sediba*.

Darryl de Ruiter of Texas A&M University was the lead craniodental specialist who helped determine the gender and age of the remains. He says the skulls are human-like but smaller, and their teeth are similar to human teeth.

"What we have here is a clearly transitional form," de Ruiter said. "We actually think we have found the best candidate for a direct ancestor of Homo, the genus to which humans belong."

What these scientists won't do to prove creation a lie.

Today, with all the technology and stuff, people can't run and hide like they did at one time. The world is being closed off, and movement suppressed for the end world government. Spy satellites can pick up things with Infrared Sensors.

Ultraviolet Sensors, Radar Sensors. Satellites can see through buildings, deep underground; last time I checked, they could see one hundred feet below the ground. **Technology keeps increasing, so who really knows what they can do and not tell us.**

CHAPTER 44

ALL ABOUT FATHER

I'M SURE THERE ARE MANY MORE VERSES THAT THEY CHANGED FATHER FOR WITH LIKE GOD. I'M GOING TO STUDY MORE ON THIS SUBJECT AND UPDATE THIS STUDY WITH WHAT I FIND IN ANOTHER LATER BOOK.

JOHN 14:9

9 Immanuel saith unto him, Have I been so long time with you, and yet hast thou not known me, Philip? he that hath seen me hath seen the Father; and how sayest thou then, Show us the Father?

Colossians 1:15

Who is the IMAGE OF THE INVISIBLE YAHWEH, the firstborn of all creation; Yahweh planted Joseph's seed in Mariam without her ever having a sexual relationship with Joseph. Immanuel was Joseph's biological son, just like the rest of Joseph's and Mariam's children. Yahweh used Immanuel for his purpose and, through the Spirit, raised him to do his will without any transgressions. To become the flesh of His Spirit fully. Yahweh took on the Flesh to become the offered Lamb. Immanuel became Yahweh's Messiah, the Father in the Flesh.

Immanuel was not crucified. He was beaten to within an inch of his life, then hung by his wrists with rope from an Olive tree until he gave up the Spirit and died. When he said, "Eli, Eli, lema sabachthani?" I believe that he felt the Spirit leaving him because Yahweh had to take His Spirit so the flesh could die.

MATTHEW 27:46

"And about the ninth hour Immanuel cried with a loud voice, saying, Eli, Eli, lama sabachthani? That is to say, My God, my God, why hast thou forsaken me?"

IMMANUEL WOULD NEVER HAVE USED THE WORD "GOD." HE WOULD HAVE SAID, MY אָב (AB) FATHER, MY אָב (AB) FATHER, WHY HAS THOU FORSAKEN ME?

HOW DID HE TEACH THEM TO PRAY?

THE "OUR FATHER" PRAYER OUR FATHER WHICH ART IN HEAVEN, RIGHTEOUS BE THY NAME THY KINGDOM COME THY WILL BE DONE IN EARTH AS IT IS IN HEAVEN. ETC.

HE DID NOT SAY, OUR GOD WHICH ART IN HEAVEN!

IN THE Garden of Gethsemane, HE PRAYED TO THE FATHER!

Matthew 26:39,42

39 After walking a little farther, he quickly bowed with his face to the ground and prayed, "Father, if it's possible, let this cup of suffering be taken away from me. But let your will be done rather than mine."

42 Then he went away a second time and prayed, "Father, if this cup cannot be taken away unless I drink it, let your will be done."

WHAT HE TOLD HIS MOTHER:

Luke 2:49:

And he said unto them, How is it that ye sought me? Wist ye not that I must be about my Father's business?

John 5:43:

I come in my Father's name, and ye receive me not: if another shall come in his own name, him ye will receive.

John 14:9:

Anyone who has seen Me has seen the Father.

John 10:30:

I and the Father are one.

MARK 14:36

And he said, Abba, Father, all things are possible unto thee; take away this cup from me: nevertheless, not what I will, but what thou wilt.

Romans 8:14

For as many as are led by the Spirit of Yahweh, they are the sons of Yahweh.

JOHN 5:17

But Immanuel answered them, My Father worketh hitherto, and I work.

JOHN 14:11

Believe me that I am in the Father, and the Father in me: or else believe me for the very works' sake.

JOHN 17:1

These words spake Immanuel, and lifted up his eyes to heaven, and said, Father, the hour is come; esteem thy Son, that thy Son also may esteem thee:

JOHN 20:17

Immanuel saith unto her, Touch me not; for I am not yet ascended to my Father: but go to my brethren, and say unto them, I ascend unto my Father, and your Father; and to my God, and your God. <-- This was added

1 Corinthians 3:17

If any man defile the house of Yahweh, him shall Yahweh destroy; for the house of Yahweh is righteous, which house ye are.

Revelation 21:7

He that overcometh shall inherit all things; and I will be his Father, and he shall be my son, and to my Father, and your Father. and *to* my God, and your God. This above verse also proves that Yahweh Messiah is the Father in the flesh and *to* my God, and your God. <-- that was added to the verse.

John 14:6

Immanuel saith unto him, I am the way, the truth, and the life: no man cometh unto the Father, but by me.

Isaiah 40:28

Hast thou not known? Hast thou not heard that the everlasting Father, Yahweh, the Creator of the ends of the earth, fainteth not, neither is weary? There is no searching of his understanding.

"IT IS NOT MY WAY OR YOUR WAY, BUT YAHWEH,

HE IS THE WORLD'S TRUE MESSIAH AND CREATOR"

PSALMS 68:11

YAHWEH GAVE THE WORD, GREAT WAS THE COMPANY OF THOSE THAT PUBLISHED IT.